STAMPING
MADE EASY

OTHER BOOKS AVAILABLE FROM CHILTON
Robbie Fanning, *Series Editor*

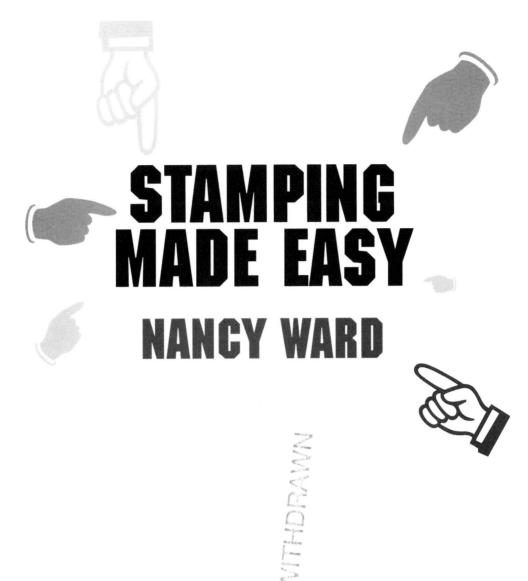

STAMPING MADE EASY

NANCY WARD

☛ CRAFT
KALEIDOSCOPE

☛ CHILTON
BOOK
COMPANY

RADNOR
PENNSYLVANIA

Designed by Adrianne Onderdonk Dudden
Drawings by Marianne Russell
Manufactured in the United States of America

Instructions and materials included in this book have been thoroughly
tested. However, no warranty, expressed or implied, is made.
Successful results are not guaranteed. Any liability for results or
accidents is disclaimed.

Library of Congress Cataloging in Publication Data
Ward, Nancy
    Stamping made easy / Nancy Ward.
      p.   cm.—(Craft kaleidoscope)
    Includes bibliographical references and index.
    ISBN 0-8019-8506-4 (pbk.)
    1. Rubber stamp printing.   I. Title.   II. Series.
TT867.W37   1994
761—dc20   93-46572
                                     CIP

1 2 3 4 5 6 7 8 9 0   3 2 1 0 9 8 7 6 5 4

The following companies provided stamps and supplies to be used in this book.
© Ad-Lib 1993
© All Night Media, Inc.
© Judith Barker and American Traditional
© Calico Cat Country Collection 1994, a division of Majorstamps
© Calico Cat Victorian Romance Collection 1994, a division of Majorstamps
© Clearsnap, Inc.
© Comotion Rubber Stamps, Inc.
© Craft House Corporation
© Kate Darnell 1992/Toomuchfun Rubberstamps, Inc.
© 1993 Delafield Stamp Company, Ltd.
© Good Stamps.Stamp Goods
© Great Notions Rubber Stamps 1994
© 1993 Hampton Art Stamps, Inc.
© 1994 Cynthia Hart; Made under license by Rubber Stampede
Copyright © ImaginAir Designs 1994
© 1994 Imprints Graphic Studio, Inc.
© 1994 Imprints Graphic Studio Canada, Inc.
© Copyright INKADINKADO, Inc.
Magna-Stamp © Clearsnap, Inc.
© Mail Order Marking/M.O.M. 1992
© Mostly Animals
© Museum of Modern Rubber
© 100 Proof Press 1993
© Pelle's See-Thru Stamps
© P.O. Box Rubberstamps 1993
© 1994 Posh Presents; Made under license by Rubber Stampede
© Quarter Moon Rubber Stamps
© Raindrops on Roses 1993
Rainy Day Stamps © 1993 Patty Schmidt and First Impression Rubber Stamp
    Arts
© Ranger Industries, Inc.
Rollagraph Stamp Wheel © Clearsnap, Inc.
© 1994 Rubber Stampede
Stamp & Design © All Night Media, Inc.
© Stamp-A-Quilt For Fabric 1994, a division of Majorstamps
© 1994 Stamp Affair
© Stamp Craft, a division of All Night Media
© 1993 Stampendous, Inc.
Stuck on Stamps Copyright 1993 by Carda International, Inc.
Works of Heart ©

Stamps on the cover: castle, © 1993 Delafield Stamp Company, Ltd.; check-
ered birdhouse, © Raindrops on Roses 1993; Christmas ball ornament, Stuck
on Stamps Copyright 1993 by Carda International, Inc.; fingerprint, © Mail
Order Marking/M.O.M. 1992; coyote, © Great Notions Rubber Stamps 1994;
musical teddy, © Mostly Animals; Ooh! Baby!, Stuck on Stamps Copyright
1993 by Carda International, Inc.; paw print, © P.O. Box Rubberstamps 1993;
Santa Smiley, © Quarter Moon Rubber Stamps.

POUR VOUS

This book is dedicated with love to three very special women:
my mother, Doris Ward;
my sister, Sally Luth;
my daughter, Kate Gillen.

CONTENTS

APPENDIX C

APPENDIX D

APPENDIX E

APPENDIX F

APPENDIX G

BIBLIOGRAPHY   107

INDEX   109

FOREWORD

The mail tumbles into our office by the sackful and I've noticed a trend in the last years: envelopes decorated by stamped images. People stamp funny messages like "100% guaranteed overdue thanks" and whimsical images like goofy cats (especially cats).

I've seen stamped clothing, too—vests, scarves, overalls, hats (many have cats on them).

Now Nancy Ward shows us how to stamp almost anything—paper, fabric, wood, clay, even Pet Rocks (but not cats).

As in *Fabric Painting Made Easy,* I admire the useful tidbits that Nancy shares: make an easy fusible patch by stamping on mending tape; plastic collar stays spread gluestick better than anything; for a fast Halloween mask, you can even stamp faces (cat faces, no doubt). Since I'm word-based, I intend to stock up on stamp supplies for do-it-yourself postcards, knowing that if I can't find the right stamp locally, I can pursue her excellent mail-order list.

From reading this book, I see that a stamp exists somewhere for every whim. What's yours? Get ready for stamping fun.

Robbie Fanning
Series Editor

Stuck on Stamps Copyright 1993 by Carda International, Inc.

P.S.
Are you interested in a quarterly newsletter about the creative uses of the sewing machine, serger, and knitting machine? Write to *The Creative Machine*, PO Box 2634, Menlo Park, CA 94026.

ACKNOWLEDGMENTS

Editors are the unsung heroines and heroes in this book-writing business. I don't envy their responsibilities. Robbie Fanning, Troy Vozzella, and Susan Keller did an outstanding job of fitting one very fat manuscript between the covers of this book.

I can't tell you what a pleasure it was working with Robbie. She is as delightful as you imagine her to be when you read her articles and books. Add that charm to her exceptional editing talents, and it's a hard combination to beat.

Two other authors who wouldn't disappoint their fans are Mary Mulari and Pele Fleming. This fan had the added advantage of gaining from their knowledge and expertise—they both were a constant source of support and information.

Joyce Whipple's input was invaluable. She went through the instructions to make sure I'd said what I wanted to say. Most friends would run and hide if asked to do this chore.

My son Jack lives in Albuquerque. He's a single parent with three young children, Alli, Jack, and Tyson. Normally a mother would be doing everything possible to help him out. Normal doesn't apply in this case. *He*, on the other hand, did everything possible to help *me* out—including bringing dinners over when I

was struggling to meet a deadline. (I can't remember the last time I cooked a meal for him and the children.)

My other sons (Dave, Tim, Joe, and Andrew), their wives (Sue, Roxane, Gina), and their children (David, Kirsten, Margaret, Ruth Ann, Harry, Timmy), and my daughter, Kate, are scattered in Michigan, Florida, and Canada. Those miles didn't stop any of them from helping out in more ways than you can imagine.

To all these wonderful people

Both Stamps © Raindrops on Roses 1993

Contributing Companies and Manufacturers

My deepest thanks to the following companies and manufacturers who provided supplies and the answers to dozens and dozens of questions for this book:

Accent, HPPG Division of Borden; Adhesive Technologies, Inc.; Aleene's; All American Graphics; Alpel Publishing; Alpha Shirt Company; American Art Clay Company, Inc.; Bead it!; The Beadery Craft Products; Chartpak; Clover Needlecraft, Inc.; Colortex Company; The Crowning Touch, Inc.; DecoArt; DEKA; Delta Technical Coatings, Inc.; Dizzle; Dritz Corporation; Duncan Crafts; EK Success, Ltd.; Elsie's Equisiques; F & W Publications; Fabricraft; Fiebing & Co., Inc.; Fiskars, Inc.; Gare; General Pencil Company; Paul K. Guillow, Inc.; Joe E. Hicks, Inc.; Jo Sonja's Artist Colors; Kemper Tools & Doll Supplies; Kony Bond; McGill, Inc.; Mark Publishing; Marvy Uchida of America Corporation; Mary's Productions; Master Magnetics, Inc.; Olfa Products Corporation; Open Chain Publishing Company; Palmer Paint Products; Pearl Paint Co., Inc.; Pebeo; Plaid Enterprises, Inc.; Polyform Products; Putnam Company; Quilter's Rule International; Riverside Paper Co.; Rowoco; Running Press; Rupert, Gibbon & Spider; Sakura; SASCO Supplies, Inc.; Sax Arts & Crafts; Savoir Faire; Sew-fit; Shepherd Hardware Products, Inc.; Specialty Ink Co.; Stencil House; Stewart Superior; Sure-Fit Designs; The Testor Corporation; Therm O Web; Tower Hobbies; Viking Sewing Machine Company; Wagner Spray Tech Corporation; West Mountain Gourd Farm; Westrim Crafts, Inc.; Wildflowers of Western Australia, Inc.; Wilton Enterprises; Yasutomo and Company (Y & C); and Z-Barten Productions.

Trademarks

The following are trademarks or registered trademarks:

®Products
Accent
All Night Media® Inc.
Beadery® Craft Products, The
Bon Ami
Ceramcoat
Cernit
Clotilde, Inc.
Creatively Yours
DEKA
Dinotopia
Dizzle
Dritz
Fabricraft
Fastube

Fasturn
Faultless
Fimo
Fiskars® Inc.
Flex Plate
Friendly Plastic
Galacolor
Gare
General's
Grafix
Graphistamp
Great Notions Rubber Stamps
HeatnBond
Helmac
Inkadinkado® Inc.
Jacquard
Jo Sonja's® Artist Colors
Kemper Tools & Doll Supplies
Kimberly® WaterColor Paint Pencils
Lint Pic-Up
Liquitex
Magna-Stamp®
Marvy® Uchida
MonoKote
Mostly Animals
Olfa
Palmer® Paint Company
Plaid Stencil Decor® Dry Brush™ Stencil Paint
Pro-Mat
Quilter's Rule
Ranger Industries, Inc.
Rollagraph® Stamp Wheel
Scribbles
Stencil Magic
Sun Catchers
Teflon
"The Masters"® Brush Cleaner and Preserver
"The Masters"® Hand Soap
Threads
Top Flite
Tower Hobbies
Viking Sewing Machine Company
VWS
Wagner® Spray Tech Corporation
Wilton
Y & C

™Products
Aleene's
Bead Easy
Clearsnap, Inc.
Comotion® Rubber Stamps Inc.
Comotion® Stamp "N' Iron™ Fabric Transfer Ink
Createx Colors
DecoArt
Delta

Distlefink Designs, Inc.
Draw & Saw
FabricArts
Felt Gard
Flexible Printing Plate
Galacraft's Magic™ Transfer Medium
HeatnBond
Hot Tape
Inkadinkado® Fabric Transfer Ink™
Kiss-Off
Mail Order Marking
Peg Pop
Pelle's See-Thru Stamps™
Pen Score
Plaid Tip Pen
Punch™ Line, The

Putnam Company, The
Quilter's Rule International
Ranger Iron-On™ Fabric Transfer Ink
Soft Shapes
Special Edition
Speed Stitch
Stamp & Design
Stamp Affair
Stamp-O-Graph
Stamp-O-Round
Stuck On Stamps
Sure-Fit Designs
Tulip
Ultra Gloss
Wearable Wash

INTRODUCTION

I can't draw a thing. Nothing. (Well, that's not exactly true—I can make a duck out of a capital S.) But when I attempted this test, I flunked. The poor man looked as though he had suffered years of dental neglect.

© Museum of Modern Rubber

Unfortunately for me, everyone assumes that someone who spends as much time sewing and crafting as I do is able to draw. People are shocked if they see one of my "drawings." Then they break into gales of laughter.

Over the years I've used every supply and method available (iron-on transfers, tracings, photocopies, patterns, to name a few). I own more cookie cutters than a bakery. (Nothing is better for basic shapes.)

Then one glorious day I discovered stamp catalogs. Stamps are better than talent—they're instant art. Now I'm faced with another problem: How can I find time to use all these wonderful stamps in all the ways they can be used?

Does that mean stamping should be considered only by those of us who can't draw? Good grief, no. A print with a stamp is done in a flash. I don't care how good you are, there's no way you can draw anything that quickly. We can always add individual touches such as the way a print is colored or enhanced, combi-

"So many stamps, so little time!"

© Quarter Moon Rubber Stamps

nations with other prints, and the surface selected for printing.

And don't think only of paper when you think of stamps. You can stamp on just about any surface that's not too furry or moving too fast.

© All Night Media, Inc.

XIII

There are endless ways stamps can be used. A print can be used singularly. Several prints can be combined to create a design. Prints can be used to enhance iron-on transfers and stencils, or used as appliqués (both stitched and fused).

Children take to stamping like ducks to water. I'm not sure we adults can't take some lessons from children. They just pick up a stamp and go. It's delightful to watch them. They don't give a hoot about pleasing someone else with their design. Unfortunately, we seem to lose that perspective as we grow into adults.

The range of projects for children described in this book are as varied as those for adults. Don't overlook the projects directed toward children—they can be enjoyed by any age. Stamping is, after all, a cross-generational activity.

Doing a rebus (using stamp prints in place of words) with the help of a preschooler is fun for both of you. In fact, have a child help you with your first rebus. Children have a way of cracking rebus "writing" down to the basics.

A rebus isn't needed to describe stamping—not when this stamp is available.

One word that's missing on this stamp is speedy. Instant art is the answer for instant projects: A roller stamp quickly changes white shelf paper into decorated gift wrap (see "Wrapping Paper, Bags, and Boxes for Gifts" in Chapter 3). A couple of prints do wonders to canvas shoes (see "Good Grief, Joyce, What's That?" in Chapter 4). A print on a wooden bookend takes a minute (see "Stamping on Wood" in Chapter 5). Jewelry is created faster than you can believe when stamps are pressed into clay (see "Stamping on Clay" in Chapter 5).

If you've read my previous book, *Fabric Painting Made Easy,* you'll find some familiar names in this book. Freezer paper and cooking parchment paper continue to be two of my favorite supplies (although white tissue paper is moving rapidly up the list). Plastic food wrap still gets slapped on a damp counter to eliminate clean-up chores. Many projects use fabric paint to ink a stamp.

After reading this book, you'll agree that the instant art of stamping provides unlimited creative opportunities—for those of you who can draw, and for those of us who can't.

© 1994 Rubber Stampede

© 1994 Rubber Stampede

1

☛ STAMPING BASICS

HOW TO USE THIS BOOK

Before beginning a project, read the directions and gather the necessary supplies. The first supply is the name of a stamp company, followed by the names or descriptions of stamps from that company used for the project. Purchasing information for stamps is given in the Stamp Index, Appendix G.

You can, of course, select to use other stamps, including those you make. Appendix A describes supplies and methods for making your own stamps.

Satisfactory results depend upon your selecting an ink suitable for the surface you are stamping. Appendix B explains inks and a variety of supplies that are suitable for use as ink. Refer to Appendix B before selecting a substitute ink.

In addition to a purchased stamp pad, several supplies can be used to ink a stamp. Descriptions of those supplies are included in Appendix C.

Substitutions can also be made for other supplies. If you have any doubts that the supply will not provide satisfactory results, pretest.

In addition to substituting stamps and supplies, you can also use another technique in place of the one explained in the directions for a project. As long as the surface is the same type (i.e., porous or nonporous), techniques described in Chapters 6 and 7 are interchanagable with those in Chapters 3, 4, and 5. Rather than coloring the edge of the Hanukkah card (Chapter 3) with a gold marker, you may prefer to add a beaded edge (see Fancy Edges, Chapter 6).

A technique described for a porous surface (paper, for example) can often be used on a nonporous surface (plastic, for example). In those cases, it will be necessary to test both the supplies and technique to ensure satisfactory results.

Regardless of the type of stamp, supply, and technique you select, get in the habit of making test prints. The few minutes spent are well worth it. Before you know it, you wouldn't think of beginning a project without making a couple of test prints.

HOW TO STAMP

Stamping isn't burdened with a lot of rights and wrongs and dos and don'ts. Practice always makes perfect, but stamping doesn't require the amount of practice needed for many craft activities. You'll be doing all sorts of fancy stuff before you know it. Each day you'll think up another way to use stamps.

One set of dos and don'ts concerns copyrights. A copyright is indicated by a ©. Stamp companies get a little bent out of shape when prints of their designs are used without permission either to make money (on items that are sold, on a business card, etc.) or to be reproduced (on a photocopier, for example). It's understandable—a company spends a lot of time and money creating these designs. If you have any questions pertaining to your use of a print, it's best to contact the company.

Stamping is as easy as tapping a stamp on an inked pad (Fig. 1-1), looking at the design to make sure it's inked evenly (Fig. 1-2), positioning the stamp on the surface you're printing and applying even pressure to the back of the stamp (Fig. 1-3), and lifting the stamp from the surface (Fig. 1-4).

1

Fig. 1-1

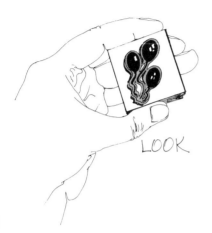

Fig. 1-2

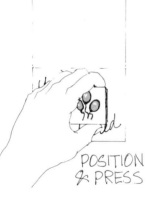

Fig. 1-3

Fig. 1-4

WHAT MAKES A STAMP A STAMP?

If you look at what is considered a traditional rubber stamp, you'll see a design (the die) that is cut from rubber and attached (mounted) to a piece of wood (the block). A layer of foam or rubber (the cushion) is between the block and die. An image (the index) of the die is printed on the back of the block (Fig. 1-5).

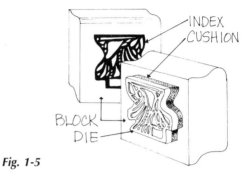

Fig. 1-5

Things have changed, however. The above description of a stamp isn't what every stamp is made from or looks like anymore. Some companies have changed our notion of what a stamp should (or must) be:

- Paint Blocks are a unique type of hardened plastic stamp. The entire front of the stamp is the design (or die). There's no worry about back prints with this stamp.

- Magna-Stamps have a magnet backing on a cushioned rubber die. The magnet attaches to a metal strip on the front of the Magna-Stamp Mount (block), which is a clear plastic box (Fig. 1-6). The blocks are available in several sizes and can be purchased separately. Instructions for use are included with purchase.

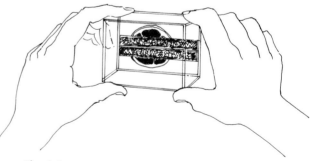

Fig. 1-6

- Pelle's See-Thru Stamps are mounted on clear Plexiglas blocks. The die is made from polymer. You're able to see through the stamp and block for easy placement when printing. Inks are quickly wiped off both die and block.

- Stuck On Stamps packaged sets have heavy-duty loop tape on the back of the rubber dies. The soft loop tape serves as a cushion. The front of the wooden blocks, which come in many sizes, are covered with heavy-duty hook tape. You can put several smaller stamps on the larger blocks and create your own designs (Fig. 1-7).

Fig. 1-7

◆ Roller stamps are available from several companies. The die is on a circular-shaped block. These stamps print a continuous design. One quick roll over an inked pad (single- or multi-color) is all it takes for a continuous line of prints. Self-inking cartridges are available for some brands of roller stamps. These cartridges can be re-inked as necessary.

◆ Then there are Sun Catchers. Some people shudder when I refer to them as stamps. But they fulfill the basic requirements of a stamp: They can be inked and the ink releases on a surface. So I call them stamps. In case you don't know what a Suncatcher is, it's a plastic form that is normally painted with glass paint (or glass stain) and hung in the window. Sun Catchers are reasonably priced and are available either in kits with paint or stain, or by the piece in bins in crafts stores. Instructions for their use are given in "Making Your Own Stamps" (Appendix A).

Dies

The die can be made from one of three products: rubber, either red, pink, or grey in color; polymer, which is a translucent plastic; or hardened plastic, which is either dark or white. Obviously a stamp does not have to have a rubber die to be a stamp.

The die should be cut deeply and evenly. Shallow-cut dies may not produce a clear print, especially on fabric. An unevenly cut die will not produce a clear print. Ideally the rubber or polymer used for the die should be trimmed close to the outer edges of the die.

There are those who would never use any type of stamp except one with a rubber die. Some wouldn't consider using a stamp unless the rubber was red or pink (no Sun Catchers for this group). Those who favor rubber think it prints better on all surfaces, produces clear prints when inked with a marker, is easier to clean, and withstands years of use.

The process of manufacturing a polymer stamp is entirely different than that used for rubber stamps,

which means that a polymer stamp produces highly detailed and intricate designs. The complaints formerly heard about polymer are things of the past, although some polymer stamps still do not ink well with markers. When it comes to cleanup time, acrylic fabric or craft paints are easily wiped off with water because they don't stick to polymer.

Hardened plastic dies are made with another manufacturing process. This type of stamp will not have a highly detailed or intricate design and most do not ink well with a marker. But they ink quickly with just about every other type of ink, and with some inks they are better than any other kind of stamp.

As far as I'm concerned, a quality polymer stamp or hardened plastic stamp is as good as a quality rubber stamp. Each type offers advantages and disadvantages. I enjoy using them all.

Cushions

Stamps often have a thin layer of foam or rubber between the stamp and the block, which is referred to as the cushion. The cushion does exactly that—it provides a cushioning effect when pressure is applied to the back of the block. The cushion also elevates the die from the front of the block. The cushion either is trimmed to the die or covers the entire front of the block (Fig. 1-8).

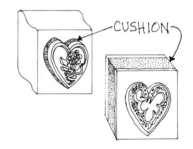

Fig. 1-8

Polymer stamps may not have a cushion layer between the die and the block. This won't present a problem when printing, unless the die has shallow cuts.

The distance between the front, or top, of the die and the block should be enough so that the front of the block will not touch the surface when a print is made (Fig. 1-9). I call that smear "back print" (see Paint Blocks in "What Makes a Stamp a Stamp?," above).

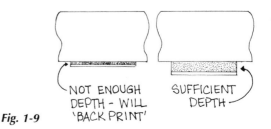

Fig. 1-9

Blocks

The stamp is attached, or mounted, to some type of backing (block) or a handle. The block will be either wood, a plastic box, clear Plexiglas or plastic, or foam. Foam blocks are either very firm or soft. Sometimes a wooden or plastic handle is used on a block or in place of a block.

Because it's impossible to produce a clear print with just the die, the block or handle is something to hang on to when you ink and then print.

Undersized stamps mounted on oversized blocks are a pain. When there's too much block extending beyond the die (and cushion), you'll have a tendency to rock the stamp back and forth when printing. Rocking or moving a stamp when printing results in smeared prints (Fig. 1-10).

Fig. 1-10

Very soft foam is spongy and bouncy. You won't have a tendency to rock stamps with a soft foam block, but you may push down too hard. Squash goes the block; squish goes the print (squish, as in all over the place). Peg Pop Mounts can be attached to the back of a foam block. The rigid plastic of the Mount helps eliminate "squishy" prints.

Mounting Supplies

Generally either rubber cement or mounting film is used as the adhesive to attach the parts of a stamp together. Both are impervious to water but not to solvent-based products. Solvent-based products (inks and cleaners) must be wiped from the die and block after use.

Index

Stamps often have an image (index) of the die on the back of the block. (You'll be looking at the index when you're printing). Some indexes are colored; some are done with black ink; some are printed on white paper that is taped to the back of the block. If the index is colored, don't think you must duplicate those colors. A colored index can give you a better idea of the print. The index may be coated with a protective finish or plastic to ensure that it will not be removed or damaged when the stamp is cleaned.

If the index does wash away, or the block does not have an index, a quick print on paper tells you what the design is. You can place that print on the back of the block and cover it with tape. Just be sure to place the index in the same direction as the die. If you don't, you could end up with a lot of upside down prints.

If the index is placed exactly over the die, it serves as a register for positioning the stamp when printing. Positioning tools are a great help when exact printing is necessary (see Chapter 6).

Stamps mounted on clear and light-colored plastic box-type blocks or solid blocks of Plexiglas usually do not have indexes.

STAMP DESIGNS

It may take some looking through stamp catalogs or stores, but any design you want is probably available. If you'd rather stamp than spend time searching for the design of your dreams, several companies make custom stamps (see Appendix G). Let them know what you want, and they will make it for you.

On the other hand, if you loved looking at Christmas catalogs when you were a child, you'll have a field day oohing and aahing over stamp catalogs. Each stamp catalog listed in Appendix G is a delight. I recommend all of them.

You can, of course, make your own stamps. Supplies and methods are explained in Appendix A, in addition to instructions for mounting unmounted stamps.

INKS

Ink is the term used for whatever substance is applied to the die. Anything can be used as long as it will coat the die—and release—when the die is placed on the surface you're printing. Descriptions of the different types of inks are given in Appendix B.

Inked pads can be purchased with either permanent or nonpermanent inks. Be sure to read the label before selecting an ink for a project. A child-safe ink pad isn't what you want to use when stamping a T-shirt. At the first washing, it's good-bye prints.

Some permanent inks are solvent-based. Solvent-based stamp cleaners must be used to clean stamps after using solvent-based inks. Read and follow all directions when using these products. Do not allow children to use them.

Re-inkers are available for just about every type of inked pad. When a pad dries out, apply more ink as directed on the re-inker bottle. Don't use one brand of re-inker on another brand of inked pad. Chances are the two brands won't be compatible.

Bottles of ink with dabber tops are also available for most types of traditional inks (Fig. 1-11). Wipe or dab the dabber top on the die. It's a good idea to pretest before beginning your project. The range of ink types, dabber tops, and dies means that not every dabber will produce the same results with every stamp on every surface.

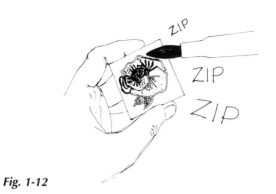

Fig. 1-11

Many products classify as nontraditional inks: glue, Texture Paste, fabric paint, glass stain, craft paints, resist, food coloring—you name it. I haven't tried chocolate pudding, but I'll bet it would work.

Nontraditional inks aren't readily available in inked pads or dabber bottles. At the present time, Fabra-ca-Dabra Acrylic Fabric Paint (see Ranger Industries, Appendix F) is the only brand available in a dabber bottle. More are on the way, but for now you'll have to ink your own pads if you use nontraditional inks, which really isn't that big of a deal. The instructions for inking pads are given in Appendix B.

Now you're wondering if you have to use these nontraditional inks. Many stampers have never considered using anything but pre-inked pads and dabber bottles. Many use only nontraditional inks. Then there are stampers like me: Sometimes I use pre-inked pads and dabber bottles; sometimes I use nontraditional inks. It depends on what I'm doing and the effect I want. Use the method that is easiest and fastest for you.

Using a marker is the speedy method of inking. It's just zip, zip across a die, and inking is done (Fig. 1-12). The surface and intended use of the finished project determine if you should use a permanent or nonperma-

Fig. 1-12

nent marker. Several brands of permanent markers are nontoxic and can be used safely by children. (The children's safety may be in danger, however, if they decide to decorate the living room walls with a permanent marker.)

Embossing ink is a specialty ink used only with embossing powders for thermal embossing. After the powder is applied to the ink, heat is used to melt the powder (see Chapter 6).

PADS

Pads hold the ink. Ideally the pad is evenly saturated with ink so that the die picks up an even layer of ink. Purchased pads are made of felt or foam and can be either inked or blank (dry).

Inked pads are available in a variety of shapes and sizes. A pad may have anywhere from one color to a dozen colors of ink. The ink is in colored bands on multi-color pads.

Dry pads are also available in a variety of sizes. Water-soluble and water-based inks can be rinsed from dry pads you've inked. With proper care, the pads last a long time.

When inking a stamp, tap it lightly on a foam pad and push it lightly on a felt pad. Because foam pads are softer than felt pads, putting too much pressure on the stamp will result in a lousy print that's surrounded by a back print (Fig. 1-13).

Fig. 1-13

Foam pads that are elevated above the base of the box can be lightly patted (not pounded) on the die. I frequently use this method of inking a die, especially those that are oversized.

There are a lot of things that can be used as substitute pads, and even more that can be used as inkers. (An inker is anything used to apply ink to a die.) These supplies often save time and/or money (see Appendix C).

SURFACES

Most surfaces are stampable. Granted, some surfaces may need to be fiddled with before you find the right ink and pad. But paper, fabric (including silk, knits, sweatshirt fleece, Ultrasuede, velvet, and felt), leather, glass, plastic, wood, plastered walls, clay, gourds, rocks, and faces are only a few of the surfaces that are easy to stamp (no more plain, unadorned Pet Rocks).

2
☛ CLEAN YOUR STAMPS!

Unfortunately, stamps are not dishwasher-safe. But the chore of cleaning them isn't as bad as you'd think. And there are reasons why it has to be done.

© 100 Proof Press 1993

- Ink must be removed from a die before inking with another color. If a stamp is re-inked on a pad of another color, the print will not be the color of that pad. For example, when a stamp with red ink is re-inked on a yellow pad, the print will be a spotty orange. The red ink also contaminates the yellow pad. Pretty soon the pad becomes a jumble of colors (none of which are yellow).

- Dried ink has a way of clogging up the fine cuts in a die. Clogged dies don't produce clear prints.

- Some inks dry rock hard. If not removed from a die immediately, they could be there forever.

After cleaning, dry and store stamps properly. See Appendix A for storage suggestions.

REMOVE INK FROM DIE BEFORE CHANGING COLORS

Remove as much ink as possible from the die. Either stamp several times on scrap paper, drag the die across paper, or wipe off the die with a piece of cotton knit fabric (my favorite) or a paper towel.

CLEAN DIES AFTER PRINTING

After removing ink from the die as directed above, clean the die with either a stamp cleaner or a damp sponge or cloth. The type of cleaner needed is determined by the type of ink (solvent-based or water-based) used.

If something should come up and you're not able to attend to cleaning immediately do the following for water-based inks: Wipe off the die. Then place the stamp, die down, on a damp sponge or towel. The remaining ink won't dry as long as it's kept damp. Clean dies within an hour. To clean, remove inks from dies with either damp paper towels or sponges, baby wipes, or purchased cleaners in a dabber bottle. After cleaning, either stamp on dry paper towels or wipe off the die and block to remove moisture.

For solvent-based inks, apply solvent-based cleaners immediately to remove these inks from stamps (and fingers). Solvent-based cleaners are available in dabber bottles.

Solvent-based cleaners can dissolve or loosen the adhesives used to mount stamps, and certain types of foam cushion are affected by solvents. That's why it's important to use a damp towel or sponge to remove all traces of the cleaners from dies and blocks after using them. After removing the cleaner, stamp on dry towels (cloth or paper) or wipe off the die and block to remove moisture.

Even if you don't use solvent-based inks, having a bottle of the cleaner in the house is a good idea. It handles all kinds of jobs. Use it to clean the stickies (glue, mounting film adhesives, etc.) off scissors blades. It removes repositionable glue, paint, and glitter from plastic stencils. It also gets rid of fusible web goofs on fabric. (Pretest fabric for colorfastness before using.)

Solvent-based products are toxic and should be kept out of the reach of children. Read and follow all directions on the label before use.

I got tired of buying products that could only be used once. It seemed that all I did was lug stuff in and haul trash out. Running to every store that had a sale on paper towels or baby wipes wasn't exactly my idea of a good time either.

After trying all kinds of substitutes, I finally had enough sense to use wedge-shaped cosmetic sponges. My lugging and hauling days are over.

Dampen several wedges with water and put them into a disposable pan that once held some sort of frozen delight (about 3″ deep × 6″ long). Also have on hand a small piece of scrap cotton knit fabric, a soft toothbrush, a couple of dry wedges, and a small container (empty yogurt containers are super) that is half-filled with plain water.

After wiping off the die with the piece of cotton knit, take a wet wedge from the pan and squeeze it almost dry. One quick wipe over the die usually removes the ink. In those few cases when it does not, use the toothbrush to gently scrub the die. Remove moisture from the die and block with a dry wedge.

Drop the inky wedge into the clean water (in the yogurt container). When finished stamping, rinse the wedges and cotton knit fabric in plain water (no soap). The inky wedges rinse clean instantly.

Removing Permanent Marker Colors from Dies

Two words handle this problem—forget it. What's not removed in normal cleaning is there to stay. The permanent ink in a marker is absorbed by both rubber and polymer dies.

This does not apply to Testors Gloss Markers, opaque or metallic. Remove these inks immediately with a solvent-based cleaner.

Cleaning Dried Ink from Stamps

If ink does dry on your stamps, either solvent-based cleaners or Kiss-Off Stain Remover will probably get them back to their original shine. ("The Master's" Brush Cleaner and Preserver can be substituted for Kiss-Off Stain Remover.)

To use solvent-based cleaners to remove dried ink, dab the cleaner on the die and gently scrub the die with a soft toothbrush.

To use Kiss-Off Stain Remover to remove dried ink, lather up a wet, soft toothbrush with the remover and gently scrub the die.

If the die is impacted with dried ink, it may be necessary to gently pick it out with a rubber gum stimulator (look for them next to the toothpaste in the drug or grocery store) after applying a solvent-based cleaner (Fig. 2-1).

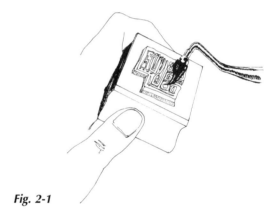

Fig. 2-1

After cleaning, remove cleaners from die and block with a damp sponge or towel (cloth or paper). Dry die and block.

© Quarter Moon Rubber Stamps

3

☞ STAMPING ON PAPER

Stamps have been used on paper for a long time, but the ways in which they're used have gone through some changes. There was a time when a stamp was thought of as only a handy time-saving tool. (It takes a lot less time to stamp "paid" on a bill than to write it.) But stamps are no longer limited to "paid" and "pay now." And paper has never looked so good.

TIPS FOR STAMPING ON PAPER

- On foam pads, lightly tap stamp; on felt pads, lightly push stamp down. Foam pads can also be patted on the die.

- Place the paper on a hard, flat surface when printing.

- Prints made with pigment ink on nonabsorbent paper (paper with a shiny or slick finish, for example) may require thermal embossing (see Chapter 6). Some pigment inks will not dry on nonabsorbent paper.

- The need to add a protective coating or surface over nonpermanent supplies (inks, markers, colored pencils, etc.) is determined by the intended use of the completed project.

- Wait until ink, markers, glue, or finishes are dry before proceeding to the next step. Taco shell holders or dish drainers work well as drying racks. A heat gun can also be used to dry inks.

- Keep hands and work tables clean to reduce the chance of smudges and smears. Master's Hand Soap quickly removes ink from hands and stamps.

Baby wipes also remove ink from fingers, hands, and work tables.

- Sometimes masking tape will pick up smudges and smears. If they won't budge, you can print a design over them or cover them with glitter paint or an opaque marker.

FOLDING, CREASING, AND CUTTING PAPER

Place the paper on a hard surface when marking, scoring, folding, or creasing. Mark the paper lightly with a soft lead pencil. When scoring marked lines, use a Clover "Hera" marker or dry ballpoint pen before creasing or folding to ensure accuracy. To prevent pressure marks, cover the paper used in the project with scrap paper before rolling pencils or skewers over folds or creases.

Remember to place a cutting mat under the paper when cutting with a craft knife or rotary cutter.

GETTING STARTED

A technique used for a project is not limited to that project. And stamps used for a project are not limited to that technique. Switch things around to your heart's content. For example, use the techniques described for the Easter card to make a Christmas card.

Colored pencils and oil pastel sticks can often be substituted for markers in paper projects. Pretest these to see which works best for you.

Many techniques described in Chapter 6 can be substituted for those used for one of the following projects. Also, refer to Appendix D for descriptions of various papers.

Do some test prints. Test prints can usually be done on scrap paper: the back of computer paper that's been through the printer, used envelopes, old file folders, torn gift boxes, yesterday's newspaper, etc. Give junk mail a purpose—use it for test prints. Whenever possible use a paper that is similar to the paper being used in the project.

© Mail Order Marking 1992

GREETING CARD PROJECTS

☛ *Note:* Supplies listed are for cards only; envelopes can be purchased or made. Instructions for making envelopes are given in "Glue It" in Chapter 7.

Easter

This will fit into a business-size envelope ($4\frac{1}{8}'' \times 9\frac{1}{2}''$).

Supplies

Mostly Animals: Aquarium Grass; Bunny Egg

Marvy Uchida Craft Punch: Bunny Punch

One $9'' \times 12''$ piece of paper (Artist Sketch, Artist Sketch Vellum or Drawing)

Ruler

Pencil or skewer

Mask for Bunny Egg (optional, see "Masking" in Chapter 6)

Small cube-size pad of green pigment ink

Yasutomo & Co. Multi-Color Stamp Pad with five pastel colors (or pad with narrow color bands)

Marker glue or glue stick (see Appendix F, Supply Sources)

Scrap paper

Directions

1 Measure 4″ down one long edge of the paper and make a very light mark. Measure 4″ down from that mark and make another light mark. Do the same on the other long edge.

2 Connect the two marks that are 4″ from the top edge by lightly drawing a line across the paper. Connect the two marks that are 4″ from the bottom edge the same way. The sheet of paper is now divided into three $9'' \times 4''$ sections.

3 Place a ruler on the top line. Hold the top section up with your left hand so that it is perpendicular to the table. Hold the ruler firmly on the paper. Run the front of your right thumbnail along the back of the top section, pushing it against the straight edge (Fig. 3-1). Turn the paper around and repeat on the bottom line. There will be a light crease on each of the two marked lines.

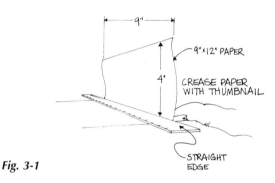

Fig. 3-1

4 Lay the paper flat on the table. Fold the top section toward the other two sections. Turn the paper over. Fold the bottom section over the folded sections. Roll a pencil or skewer over the fold lines to flatten the fold so that the card lies flat. Open the paper flat, wrong side up.

5 There will be two creased lines on the paper. The creases divide the paper into three sections. The lower section is the front of the card (Fig. 3-2).

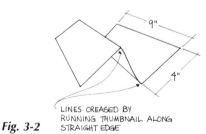

Fig. 3-2

6 Ink the Bunny Egg stamp on the five-color pad. Place the prints on the bottom section of the paper, on the wrong side of the paper, below the fold line (Fig. 3-3). Fill the front of the card with prints. Use a mask or place the prints next to each other. Ink each time you print. The bands of ink in a Y & C

Fig. 3-3

Multi-Color Stamp Pad are narrow. Each egg print will have three bands of colors.

7 Slide a piece of scrap paper under the lower edge of the paper (the one with the egg prints). Ink just the top half of the Aquarium Grass stamp with the green pigment ink pad. Print along the lower edge of the paper, over the egg prints (Fig. 3-4). (It'll look like the eggs are sitting in tall grass.) Remove the scrap paper when finished printing.

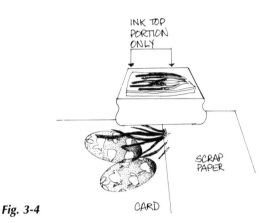

Fig. 3-4

8 Turn the paper over, print side down. Apply marker glue or glue stick around the bottom edge and both sides of the lower section. Lift the lower section over the middle section. Finger press in place.

9 Punch bunny shapes along the lower edge, above the creased fold line. The bunnies don't have to be in a straight row or evenly spaced from one another (Fig. 3-5). (These are happy, hoppy bunnies!)

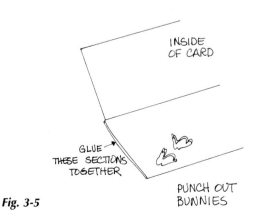

Fig. 3-5

10 Fold the printed section down—you've made an Easter card.

Variations and Suggestions for Easter Card Stamps and Punches

♦ Do not glue edges together (step 8). Punch bunny shapes in the card as directed in step 9. Put colored paper, ribbon, mylar, or fabric between the middle and bottom section of the card. Then glue the edges. The colored paper (ribbon, etc.) will show through the punched design.

♦ Print the Bunny Egg on any type of paper. Make and cut out several prints. Use marker glue to glue the two prints together, print sides out. Cover both sides of the egg prints with adhesive vinyl, leaving a tiny tab of vinyl on the top of the egg. Thread a needle and push it through the tab. Tie the ends of the thread together. Find a good-looking branch. As an option, paint it with glitter paint. Stick the branch into a hunk of clay placed in the bottom of a small clay pot. Hang the eggs from the Easter Egg tree. Use mylar or tissue paper "grass" to cover the clay.

♦ Print the design used on front of card (eggs and grass) on a T-shirt.

Halloween

Supplies

Comotion Rubber Stamp Company: Jumbo Pumpkin; Fred A Scare (skeleton); Happy Halloween

One 9″ × 12″ piece of orange construction paper (either the inexpensive type used for school projects or the more expensive type with a smooth finish)

One 3″ × 3½″ piece of silver origami paper (silver wrapping paper or silver lamé fabric can be substituted)

Pencil or skewer

Craft knife or scissors

Dark green marker and dark orange marker (permanent or nonpermanent)

Marker glue or glue stick

Stamp pad with black ink (either dye-based or pigment ink)

Embossing pen or erasable ballpoint pen

Black embossing powder

Heat source for melting embossing powder

Scrap paper

☛ *Note:* Read about thermal embossing in Chapter 6 before beginning.

Directions

1 Fold the orange paper in half, long edges together. Roll a skewer or pencil over the fold line.

2 Open the paper and fold it in half, this time with the short edges together. Roll a skewer or pencil over the fold line. Do not open the paper.

3 Print the Jumbo Pumpkin between the crease made in step 1 and the right edge of the card.

4 Open the paper, pumpkin print up. Use scissors or a craft knife to cut out the eyebrows, eyes, nose, and mouth from the pumpkin print (Fig. 3-6).

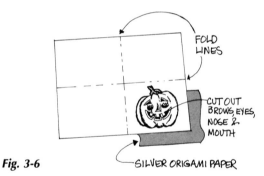

Fig. 3-6

5 Turn the paper over. Apply a light coating of glue around the edges of the cut openings. Apply a light coating of glue around the outer edges of the silver origami paper.

6 Position the silver paper behind the cut openings. Use your fingers to press it securely on the construction paper.

7 Color the stem of the pumpkin with a dark green marker. Color the areas surrounding the facial features with a dark orange marker.

8 Fold the paper in half, long edges together. The side with the pumpkin print will be face down. The inside of the card is up, with the fold line at the top.

9 Beginning at the lower left-hand corner, lightly draw a pencil line across the card to the upper right-hand corner of card. Draw two parallel lines, one 2″ above and one 2″ below the first line.

10 Place the card on a piece of scrap paper that is larger than the card. Position the skeleton stamp on the middle line so that the lower left corner of the block is on the lower left corner of the card. A portion of the left side of the print will be on the scrap paper under the card.

11 Reposition the skeleton stamp on the card so that the left side of the block is next to the foot of the first skeleton on the middle line. Print across the entire middle line using the foot of the skeleton and the marked line as position guides. Most of the print in the upper right-hand corner of the card will be on the scrap paper (Fig. 3-7). Print across the lower line, using the same method.

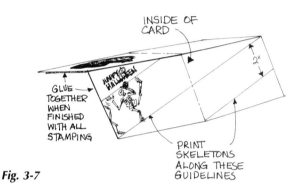

Fig. 3-7

12 Print Happy Halloween in the upper left-hand corner of card. The bottom of the block should be on the top line.

13 Open the card. The pumpkin and skeleton prints are down. Apply a thin layer of glue to the edges of the bottom half of the card. Fold the top half over. The skeleton and Happy Halloween prints will be up. Finger press the outer edges to secure the glue. When the glue has dried, roll a pencil or skewer over the folded edges of the card.

14 Sign the card with an embossing pen. Emboss with black embossing powder.

Variations and Suggestions for Halloween Card Stamps

▸ Print stamps of your choice, using opaque white fabric paint as the ink, on black T-shirts or sweatshirts. Paint the pumpkin with either opaque orange, metallic orange, or fluorescent orange fabric paint. Dry flat. Apply permanent glue to the facial features of the pumpkin. Sprinkle glow-in-the-dark glitter over the glue. Dry flat for at least four hours. Roll Lint Pic-Up over the shirt to remove excess glitter. Do not launder the shirt for two weeks.

▸ The Jumbo Pumpkin stamp can be used on shrink plastic for buttons and earrings. Follow the manufacturer's directions for use on plastic.

◆ Have children print the stamps on shopping bags to use for Trick or Treat.

◆ Children can print the skeleton on the paper insert of a plastic badge or button makers.

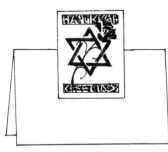

Hanukkah

Supplies

Stuck On Stamps: Hanukkah Greetings, large

Blank note card, single fold

Gold pigment pad

Gold Tinsel or Foil Embossing Powder

Craft knife and cutting mat

Gold marker

Heat source for melting embossing powder

☛ *Note:* Read "Pop-Ups," "Thermal Embossing," and "Fancy Edges" in Chapter 6 before printing card.

Directions

1 Open the card flat, right side up.

2 Ink the stamp. Print over the fold line so that the top half of the print is on the card back and the bottom half of the print is on the card front.

3 Sprinkle embossing tinsel over the ink. Shake off the excess powder. Heat to melt the powder.

4 Place the card on a cutting mat. Open the card flat, right side up. Use a craft knife to cut along the outer edges of the top half of the print on the card back. Do not cut below the fold line on the card front.

5 Run a gold marker along the outer edges of the card.

Variations and Suggestions for Hanukkah Card Stamp

◆ Purchase a flat wooden plaque in a crafts store. After sanding, brush a thin coat of white paint (diluted fabric paint or diluted acrylic craft paint) over all sides. When dry, print with a gold paint (fabric or craft paint or Jo Sonja's Artist Color Acrylic Paint). Apply a hanger to back of the plaque.

◆ Roll white clay that requires oven baking out to ½" thickness on a piece of cooking parchment paper (see "Stamping on Clay" in Chapter 5). Print in the clay. Cut away the excess clay from the outer edges of the print. Sprinkle gold Tinsel or Foil Embossing Powder over the print. Brush off the excess powder. Bake according to the manufacturer's directions. (Leave the clay on the cooking parchment paper for baking and cooling.) When cool, attach a hanger to the back of the clay.

Christmas and Valentine's Day

☛ *Note:* Cards for these occasions are included in "Valentine Gift Wrap" and "Christmas Box" later in this chapter (see "Stamping on Wood" in Chapter 5 for Valentine Cube).

DECORATED ENVELOPES

Some people think that a plain envelope is like a horse without a shoe. So it's no surprise that there's a type of stamp referred to as a "stamp frame." The frame surrounds the stamp that gets our mail through hail, sleet, rain, and snow. Inkadinkado has two stamp frames, Sunny Day Stamp Frame and Snowflakes Box Stamp Frame, that look great around a postage stamp. Patting a small pad on selected areas of the die allows for printing options.

Sunny Day has four print options: the stamp frame, the sun and large clouds, the flowers across the bottom, and the little flower (Fig. 3-8, © Inkadinkado, Inc.).

Fig. 3-8

Snowflakes has two print options: the stamp frame and a single line of snowflakes for background printing.

Either stamp can be used to print the same frame in the right-hand corner of an envelope and/or to print selected portions of the die all over the envelope.

Stamp frames aren't the only type of stamp offering multiple print options. In several cases, patting ink on selected portions of the die is faster than masking (see "Masking" in Chapter 6).

STICKER PROJECTS

Stickers can be placed on any surface that will not be laundered or harmed by the glue on the sticker. Most stickers are removable, but check the label to make sure. If you can't find them in a stamp store or catalog, go to an office-supply store. They have stickers in a zillion sizes and shapes, including $8\frac{1}{2}'' \times 11''$ sheets of uncut sticker paper.

© Comotion Rubber Stamps, Inc.

For the Teacher

A box of these stickers are a great Christmas gift for the teacher in your child's life.

Supplies

Comotion Rubber Stamps, Inc.: Excellent!; Good Job

Small square and rectangular stickers

Black pigment-ink pad

Red and blue markers (colored pencils can be substituted)

Directions

1 Print Good Job on the square stickers. Print Excellent! on the rectangular stickers. Allow the ink to dry.

2 Color the prints with markers.

Variations and Suggestions for Stamps

▶ If you're a teacher, you know how handy these stamps are on homework papers.

▶ Print Excellent! on a child's baseball cap (Fig. 3-9), tennis shoes, a shirt, or all of them. A shirt covered

Fig. 3-9

with this print belongs in every child's wardrobe (see Chapter 4 on how to stamp on fabric).

Chore Calendar

The hassle of the daily chore list is made a lot easier with these stamps. Get a calendar for everyone you know in the household work force (Fig. 3-10). Print the jobs that apply to your household on stickers. If you print several sets at one time, keep each set separate. Decide which day of the week is "Pull Your Chore Out of the Bag Day." What they grab is their chore for the next week. (Then you won't be blamed for who gets what.) The sticker goes on the calendar, and all the chores get done with a smile (don't you wish?).

Fig. 3-10

Supplies

Mostly Animals: Charting My Chores Kit

Calendars

Small stickers

Grab bag (paper lunch bag, something fancier if you wish)

Directions

1 Mount the stamps. (Dies, blocks, and an inked pad are included in kit.)

2 Print on the small stickers.

3 Put the stickers in a bag and let the fun begin.

Variations and Suggestions for Stamps

♦ Print on small wooden blocks. Use the blocks in the grab bag. Hand write chores on the calendar.

♦ Make an apron using checked gingham fabric with $1/2''$ squares. The prints fit perfectly in the white squares. Use a Dritz Apron Clip to make a speedy, no-sew apron. The clips are found in the Dritz display in fabric stores.

♦ These are handy stamps for children to use in stamp books (see "Stamp Books" later in this chapter).

© 1993 Stampendous, Inc.

Decorating Packages

Tape doesn't deter the really curious types at gift time. I know. My daughter figured out early in life how to peel it off so that her peeking would go unnoticed. Permanent stickers are peel-proof; they keep the curious Kates in check.

Supplies

Stampendous: No shakin' pokin' or peekin!! (Don't open until Christmas, Small Star Stripe, and Bold Star Stripe)

Small permanent stickers (or leftover computer labels)

Pigment-ink pad (single or multi-color)

Directions

1 This is as easy as it gets. Ink the stamps and print. Needless to say, these are great stamps to use for repeat prints on plain wrapping papers.

Variations and Suggestions for Stickers

♦ Ever so lightly mark 1" squares on a sheet of sticker paper. Make one print in each square. Use an Olfa perforated blade in a rotary cutter to cut along the marked lines. If you don't have these tools, set your sewing machine on a narrow buttonhole stitch to "stitch" (don't thread the machine) the lines. Then pull the sections apart. (A straight stitch can be substituted for the buttonhole stitch.)

♦ These stamps won't carry the mail, but you can imagine all the uses they have: on the back of an envelope; in children's sticker books; as pleasant reminders (Fig. 3-11, © Ad-Lib 1993); as unpleasant reminders; on lunch bags; or for making your very own Elvis stamp.

Love you!

Fig. 3-11

WRAPPING PAPER, BAGS, AND BOXES FOR GIFTS

Tissue paper and shelf paper are inexpensive supplies to use when printing gift wrap. Bond freezer paper to tissue paper when a strong or opaque paper is needed. To do this, place freezer paper, shiny side down, on the tissue paper. Press with an iron at a silk setting. Allow the paper to cool before removing it from the board.

Waxing also makes tissue paper stronger and a heavy layer of wax can make colored tissue waterproof. Cover the ironing board with white tissue paper. Lay a piece of wax paper on the tissue paper. Cover with the tissue paper to be waxed; place another piece of wax paper on top of this tissue paper. Press at a wool setting. Turn the papers over. Press on that layer of wax paper. Remove all papers from the ironing board when cool.

The heat of the iron melts the wax, which is absorbed by the tissue paper. Use fresh wax paper for each piece of tissue paper. (There's not a lot of wax on wax paper.)

Either of these methods can be done before or after printing and coloring with permanent inks and markers. Watercolor markers and inks should be used *before* waxing. Prints made with pigment ink should be thermal embossed if tissue paper is waxed. Papers using either of these methods can be pressure embossed.

Shelf paper is inexpensive. Newsprint is even less expensive (especially if it's free—check with your local newspaper). A roller stamp with an inking cartridge and either of these papers creates terrific, low-cost gift wrap in minutes.

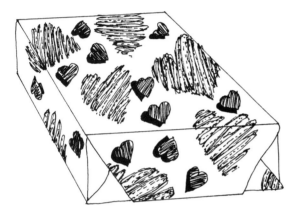

Valentine Gift Wrap

Supplies

Comotion Rubber Stamps, Inc.: Jumbo Brush Heart; Small Brush Heart

Pencil

Sheet of pink pearlized tissue paper in size needed for gift box (Coated tissue papers, like pearlized, do not need to be waxed or bonded to freezer paper.)

Scissors

Small silver pigment-ink pad

13½″ × 13½″ Sheet of adhesive vinyl

Double-faced tape

2″ × 2″ piece of freezer paper

Embossing pen (optional)

Silver embossing powder (optional)

Directions

1   Open the sheet of tissue paper and smooth flat, right side down. Place the gift box on the paper. Measure the size of the paper needed to wrap the box. Cut the paper to the measurements. Save the remaining paper.

2   Turn the paper over, right side up. Pat the ink cube on the large heart stamp. Print the design randomly on the paper, leaving at least 4″ between each print.

3   Wrap the gift box. Use double-faced tape under the paper at the back seam and ends.

4   Pat the ink on the small heart stamp. Print several designs on the right side of the paper remaining from step 1. Let the ink dry.

5   Remove the covering from the adhesive side of the adhesive vinyl. Place the adhesive side of the vinyl on the wrong side of the paper with the small heart prints.

6   Cut out the small heart prints. Use one of the laminated hearts as a pattern to trace one heart shape on a piece of tissue paper. Bond freezer paper to the wrong side of the tissue paper. Cut out the traced heart to use as a gift tag.

7   On the gift tag, write the name on the tissue paper side with an embossing pen. Emboss with silver embossing powder. (A silver marker can be substituted for the embossing pen and powder.) Put a ¼″ piece of double-faced tape in the center of the tag, on the freezer paper side.

8   Place a ¼″ piece of double-faced tape in the center of each small heart print, on the vinyl side.

9   Attach the laminated small hearts in the spaces between the large heart prints. Attach the gift tag.

Variations and Suggestions for Heart Stamps

▸ The Jumbo Brush Heart is suitable for use on shrink plastic.

▸ Print hearts of both sizes with red ink on the front of a white T-shirt or sweatshirt.

▸ Make a pop-up (see Chapter 6) Valentine card. Bond freezer paper to the back of red wrapping tissue. Cut the paper to card size. Fold the paper in half, forming a card. Open the card flat, tissue paper side up. Print the Jumbo Heart with silver pigment ink on the fold. Cut around the edges of the print on the back of the card to make a pop-up.

▸ Use the small heart to decorate envelopes with echo prints as described in Chapter 6. Emboss with clear powder if desired.

Roller Stamps for Speedy Gift Wrap

Roller stamps decorate wrapping paper so fast that you almost have to see it to believe it. Either multi-color or single-color pads can be used for inking.

When using a multi-color pad, don't run the roller stamp back and forth over the pad, which will muddy up the colors. One pass should ink the stamp. If the colors do start to blend, wipe across the width of the pad with a dry paper towel. Don't wipe the pad from end to end—that will mix the colors more.

If you have problems tracking a roller stamp (the roller goes right when you wanted it to go left, or the lines are all over the place), use a "rolling guide" (a term I made up) on the surface—a ruler, a French curve, a piece of ⅛″-thick Plexiglas, the edge of a large bowl turned upside down, etc.—anything that will guide the stamp. Butt the edge of the stamp against the guide and away you go. Make sure that the stamp will still roll when it's against the guide. If the guide isn't too small and the stamp isn't too wide, you can even roll circular and loopy designs.

When using a roller stamp, roll across the full width or length of the paper or completely around a curved rolling guide. Stopping midstream makes for a choppy connection between prints.

If the paper (bag, box, or envelope) is very wide or the guide is large, the prints could fade away before you reach the other side. Use the junction where the two ends of the die come together as a register mark (mark the edge of the block with an opaque white marker). That junction should be in the same place on the handle or holder on the die when you begin and stop printing.

The handles used for Rollagraph Stamp Wheels are available with and without self-inking cartridges. Regardless of the type of handle used, Rollagraph Stamp Wheels can be inked on either a single- or multicolor pad. With a self-inking cartridge (Fig. 3-12), the stamp just keeps on printing, the better choice when decorating a paper tablecloth (or any wide surface) with a roller stamp design.

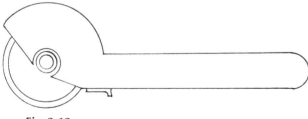

Fig. 3-12

Brown Bag It

I used to make fabric gift bags until someone was clever enough to start selling paper gift bags. Now the only time I make a fabric gift bag is when I need an odd size.

A couple of quick prints is all a gift bag needs. Stick shredded tissue or mylar, or just plain tissue, into the top to hide the goodies inside. Tie the handles together with the ribbon used on a gift tag you stamp.

When you don't have time to get to the store to buy a gift bag, and sewing isn't your thing, a brown paper lunch bag is the best substitute (Fig. 3-13).

Fig. 3-13

Supplies

Delafield Stamp Company: Baby Hugo; Cat

Marvy Uchida Black Liquid Appliqué (or your favorite color cat)

Rubber roller (brayer)

Piece of freezer paper

Brown paper lunch bag

Piece of cardboard or Plexiglas that is almost as wide as the bag

Blank index card

Heat source for puffing Liquid Appliqué (see the manufacturer's suggestions on the label)

3 yards of gift wrap or craft ribbon that curls when you pull it over the edge of a knife or scissors blade.

Double-faced tape

Directions

1 Do not open the bag. If the bag has been used, flatten along the fold lines. Slide cardboard or Plexiglas inside the bag. It should be on top of the folds inside the bag. (Printing must be done on a flat surface. If the folds aren't covered, the print will not be clear.)

2 Remove the tip from the barrel of Liquid Appliqué (turn it clockwise). Squirt some Liquid Appliqué on the shiny side of the freezer paper and roll it out. The roller should be evenly coated with a thin layer of ink.

3 Roll the ink over the Baby Hugo die. Print in the center of the bag. If you want a print on the other

side, wait at least fifteen minutes before turning the bag over and printing.

4 Re-ink the roller. Ink the Cat stamp and make several prints on index cards.

5 Puff the prints. Note: Although Marvy Uchida recommends waiting twelve hours before puffing, there are times when it's better not to wait that long. Too much puff will cover the details of this stamp, so I puff in about thirty minutes. Pretest for satisfactory results.

6 Cut out the Cat prints.

7 Curl 3 yards of ribbon (less if there's not that much on the roll). Cut off one 6″-long piece.

8 Take the pile of curled ribbon and wrap the 6″ piece around the center of the wad. (Don't fret if the tie is not exactly in the center.)

9 Put a small piece of double-faced tape on the back of each Cat print. Stick the prints on the ends of the curled ribbon, away from the center. It's O.K. if some prints stick to two widths of ribbon. Use half of the prints on one side of the tie and the other half on the other side.

10 Put the gift into the bag. Stuff curled ribbon into the top of the bag with the tied area toward the bottom. Arrange the ribbon so that the Cat prints are hanging over the top of the bag.

Variations and Suggestions for Gift Bag Stamps

Cat lovers won't have any problems coming up with uses for these stamps. Here are a few.

● Make a Baby Hugo print on a blank index card to use as a gift tag. After puffing (puff paint is optional), cut out the print. Punch a small hole in the top of the print for string.

● Print the Cat stamp on plain white buttons with a shank. Look for buttons with flat tops. Use a solvent-based ink suitable for printing on plastic. You also can print on white fabric and glue the cut-out prints to the top of button covers. Apply permanent glue over the print to seal the cut edges of the fabric.

● Print with fabric ink on T-shirts. (I'll bet you had already thought of that one.)

Christmas Box

Blank gift boxes and stamps mean no gift wrapping. You don't even have to fuss with a bow. Gift tags can be made with the same prints used on the boxes. Boxes are available in assorted shapes, sizes, and colors in crafts, art supply, and stationery stores.

Toomuchfun Rubberstamps, Inc. has an assortment of stamps in various sizes for printing boxes (and envelopes). The hardest thing about using these stamps is to avoid making the box more spectacular than the gift inside. Bond freezer paper to either origami paper or tissue paper to create low-cost beauties. Fusible web can also be used to fuse papers together. Stencils used for making boxes and envelopes are available from American Traditional (see Appendix E).

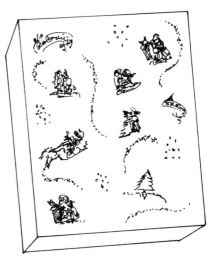

Supplies

Hampton Art Stamps: Victorian Santa; Ice Skaters; Bringing Home The Christmas Tree; Carolers; Sleigh Ride; Sand/Snow; Holiday Pine; Snow Flakes; Seasons Greetings (use as many stamps as desired)

Blank box in size needed

Red, green, and gold or multi-color pigment-ink pads (pigment ink used on shiny or glossy paper boxes must be thermal embossed)

Glitter and glue (glitter paint can be substituted)

Blank index card

Punch

Red Pearl Cotton or double-faced tape

Clear tape

Directions

1 Leave the box flattened until all the printing is completed.

2 Print the top and sides of the top. Print the bottom of the box. Do not print the sides of the bottom.

3 With glue, make random lines in and around the prints. Immediately sprinkle glitter over the glue (Fig. 3-14). Shake the excess glitter from the box when the glue is dry.

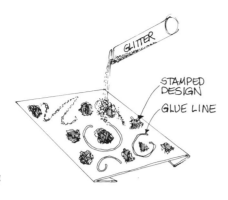

Fig. 3-14

4 Select one stamp to print on a blank index card. Either punch a hole at the top of the card for the string (Pearl Cotton) or attach the tag to the box with double-faced tape.

5 Place the gift in the box and tape the box closed.

Variations and Suggestions for Christmas Stamps

♦ Make prints in the corner of white napkins to be used for Christmas dinner.

♦ Print in clay (see Chapter 5). Attach pin backs with glue, mounting film, or mounting tape.

♦ Print on blank greeting cards. Emboss or foil edges of cards (see "Fancy Edges" in Chapter 6).

♦ Print on greeting card envelopes. Using envelope stencil as a guide, add a 1″ extension to the back flap of the envelope (see "Glue It" in Chapter 7). Print Victorian Santa (or stamp of your choice) ¼″ from lower edge of flap. Mark and cut a straight line that is 1″ up from the lower edge of the flap and ¼″ from each side of the print. Trim the lower edge of the print to ⅛″ (Fig. 3-15). Glue the envelope together.

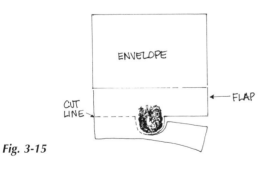

Fig. 3-15

Christmas

Teeny gift tags always seem to leave us wanting more. And I like tags that go from the present to the tree, a pleasant way to renew memories each year when the tree is decorated.

Paint Block shown 50% of actual size

Supplies

Paint Blocks: Christmas Tree or a large holiday design of your choice.)

Blank 4″ × 6″ index cards or sheet of poster board (Bristol board sheets can be substituted for heavier tags; cut as directed for poster board.)

Scissors or craft knife (rotary cutter optional)

Wedge-shaped cosmetic sponge

Green Dizzle Bright Fabric Paint for tree print; Gold and Red Dizzle Bright Fabric Paint for decorating the print

Piece of plastic food wrap

Sequins or beads (optional)

Punch (either small circle or Christmas theme)

Metallic marker

⅛″-wide ribbon in red, gold, and green

Directions

1 If using poster board or bristol board, cut square and rectangular pieces with scissors or rotary cutter in sizes needed for prints.

2 Wipe off the kitchen counter with a damp sponge. Spread the plastic food wrap on the damp counter, smoothing flat with a sponge. (The wrap will adhere to the damp surface.) Squirt a glop (about the size of a fifty-cent piece) of the green fabric paint on the plastic food wrap.

3 Ink the cosmetic wedge with paint. The layer of ink should be even and clearly visible.

4 Pat the ink evenly on the surface of the Paint Block.

5 Print on blank index card, poster board, or bristol board. Allow to dry. Repeat for the needed number of tags.

6 Using the red and gold fabric paint as glue, attach the sequins and beads as decorations on tree prints. Paint a star with gold paint.

7 Cut out the prints along the outer edges, leaving space above the star for a punched hole.

8 Punch a hole (or shape) in the top of the tags. Write the names and date on the back with a metallic marker.

9 Use ribbon to attach the tag to the gift. Hang the tag on the tree after the gift is opened.

Variations and Suggestions for Gift Tag Stamps

♦ Print on tissue paper for coordinated gift wrap. See "Wrapping Paper, Bags, and Boxes for Gifts," above for methods of strengthening and waterproofing tissue paper.

♦ Print either one design or an assortment of designs on T-shirts or sweatshirts.

♦ Print around the hem of the stapled Christmas tree skirt described in Chapter 7 (Fig. 3-16).

Fig. 3-16

♦ Read about laminated fabric in "Fuse It," in Chapter 7. Print on muslin. Laminate for sturdy place mats and a table runner.

Super Speedy Gift Tags

Go to an office-supply store where you can buy marking tags, which are price tags used by stores. The tags come in a lot of sizes and colors, including white, red, and bright yellow. The larger sizes make perfect gift tags—all they need is a print. The string is already attached.

Another speedy method is to use the Gift Tag stamp from Ad-Lib to print six tags at one time. Cut the tags apart along the marked lines of the print.

Check out crafts stores for 8″ × 11″ sheets of magnet with an adhesive backing. The sheets cut easily with scissors. Use a large stamp to print on paper, and then cover the back of the print with a magnet. Big prints mean big magnets, which means they stay in place instead of sliding down the front of the refrigerator door every time it's closed.

Inexpensive papers (typing or computer paper or blank index cards) can be used for the prints. For long-term use, cover the prints with adhesive vinyl.

Birth Announcement

Putting a birth announcement on a magnet solves a lot of problems. As soon as it's received, it'll probably go on the front of the refrigerator anyway, and no one will forget that special birthday. The announcement still may be there when that child starts school (Fig. 3-17).

Fig. 3-17

Supplies

☞ *Note:* Increase amounts of index cards, magnetic sheeting, and adhesive vinyl as required.

Delafield Stamp Company: Birth Announcement

Gold pigment-ink pad

Three 4″ × 6″ blank index cards (three prints can be put on one card)

Magnet Maker (8″ × 11″ flexible magnet with adhesive on one side; eight announcements can be put on one sheet)

Adhesive vinyl (13½″ × 13½″ sheet can be used for eighteen announcements)

Scissors

Pencil or skewer

Metallic marker

White tissue paper

Heavyweight manila or padded envelopes, 4″ × 6″

Directions

1 Ink the stamp. Make three prints on each index card. Allow to dry.

2 Remove the paper covering the adhesive side of the magnet and lay flat with short ends at the top and bottom. Position the first card on the magnet in the upper right-hand corner. Position the second card to the left of the first card. Cut the third card apart between the prints. Position the two prints across the bottom of the magnet (Fig. 3-18).

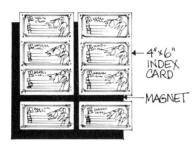

Fig. 3-18

3 Address and stamp (the kind the post office requires) the envelopes. Place the announcements and envelopes in a box until the big day.

4 After the baby arrives, use metallic marker to fill in the announcement.

5 Remove the covering from the adhesive side of the vinyl. Cover the front of the announcement with vinyl. Roll a skewer or pencil over the vinyl to attach it securely to the announcement.

6 Cut the announcements apart. Wrap each in white tissue before placing in the envelope. Then grab a nap before the baby wakes up.

Another Magnetic Suggestion

 If you have a white board that holds magnets, turn it into a toy or teaching aid by placing prints on magnetic sheeting. After losing the battle of the "sliding alphabet on the refrigerator door" for more years than I care to think about, I think this is the better way to go.

PUZZLING INVITATIONS

It's fun sending party invitations that are printed on a blank puzzle (Fig. 3-19). Break the puzzle apart after printing and then put the pieces in the envelope. You'll find out who isn't good at putting puzzles together. (They'll miss the party.)

Supplies

☛ **Note:** Puzzles can be purchased with and without envelopes (a blank envelope works fine) in crafts stores. See "Glue It" in Chapter 7 for making your own envelopes.

Fig. 3-19

Stuck On Stamps: Party Invitation Stamp Set (Let's Celebrate!, Occasion, Balloons, Streamers, and You're Invited were used.)

Blank puzzle, 5½″ × 8″

Three-color pigment-ink pad

Dark-color marker

Paper

Pencil

Blank envelopes

Directions

☛ **Note:** Print on scrap paper to make sure the stamp is positioned in the right direction. Don't break the puzzle apart until both sides have been printed. Complete all printing before cleaning the dies.

1 Place the Balloon die on the small block included in the kit. (Dies and blocks have hook-and-loop backings.) Ink the stamp on one color of the pad. Print randomly, without re-inking, until the stamp does not print.

2 Repeat step 1 with the second and third colors of ink. Continue printing until one side of the puzzle is covered with balloon prints. Wipe the ink from the die and remove from the block.

3 Place the You're Invited die on the large block included in the kit. Print in the upper right-hand corner of the puzzle, over the balloon prints. Wipe the ink from the die and remove from the block.

4 Place the Occasion die on the large block. Ink. Print in the lower left-hand corner of the stamp. Wipe the ink from the die and remove from the block. Use a dark-color marker to fill in the blanks on the Occasion print. When dry, turn the puzzle over.

5 Place the Let's Celebrate die on the large block. Place the stamp on an angle on the pad when inking. Change the angle for each inking. (Colors will be different for each print when this is done.) Print from the upper left-hand corner to the lower right-hand corner. Print at least twice before re-inking the pad. Print, using the same inking procedure, on both sides of the first line of printing. This side of the puzzle should be covered with prints. Wipe the ink from the die and remove from the block.

6   Cut a 2½″ × 3½″ piece of paper. Place it on the envelope, midway between the top and bottom, and 3″ from the right side edge. Trace lightly around the paper piece with a pencil. Cut a 1″ × 2″ piece of paper. Place it in the upper left-hand corner of the envelope front. Trace lightly around the paper piece with a pencil.

7   Place both the Balloon and Streamer dies on the large block. Print the envelope front in the same method used for step 1. Do not print within the marked lines. Turn the envelope over when the ink is dry. Print the envelope back. Wipe the ink from the dies and remove from the block.

8   In the small unprinted space in the upper left-hand corner of the envelope write the return address. In the larger unprinted space in the center of the envelope write the address.

9   Break the puzzle apart and put the pieces into the envelope.

10   Clean all dies.

Obviously the instructions are for one invitation, and most if not all parties need more than one. Print all fronts at one time, then the backs, and finally the envelopes. Have a great party!

Variations and Suggestions for Puzzle Stamps

▸   Use these stamps, as well as others included in the kit, to print on balloons and the paper napkins, cups, plates, and tablecloths used at the party.

▸   Puzzles aren't limited to party invitations. Use puzzles for printed notes and holiday greetings.

▸   Have children design and print puzzles to give as gifts.

SPECIAL GIFTS TO KEEP OR GIVE

Carousel Mobile

I won't even pretend that this is a quickie project. It won't take days, but it will take more than a couple of hours. The finished results, though, are worth every minute spent.

Don't be intimidated by the amount of instructions. I just used a lot of words to describe some simple steps. In no way should this be considered an advanced project.

Supplies

☛ *Note:* The supplies are for a large mobile with eight animals; follow the same steps to make a small mobile with fewer animals.

Mostly Animals: Carousel Animals (Camel, Lion, Bear, Horse Flyer, Armored Horse, Ostrich, Frog, Tiger); Carousel Pole; Jester Sconce; Cherub Sconce

© Mostly Animals

One 9″ wooden hoop (inner embroidery hoop or hoop used to make basket)

Gold Jo Sonja's Artist Color (optional)

Small paintbrush (only if hoop is painted)

Removable tape

Three 9″ × 12″ sheets tracing vellum

Two sheets 13½″ × 13½″ adhesive vinyl

Markers and/or pastel chalk pencils for coloring prints; at least six colors needed (Markers and pencils can be used on the same print.)

Black pigment-ink pad (a new one if possible)

Mounting film cut in ½″ strips or ½″-wide double-faced sewing/craft tape

½ yard of ½″-wide decorative ribbon

Clear nylon thread or fine nylon fishing line

Small snap swivel (purchased in sporting goods store)

French crimp (a jewelry item that can be purchased in most crafts stores)

Pliers (needle-nosed if possible)

Stamp-O-Graph or other positioning tool. (A printing tool is optional and is used for reprinting the print after coloring, see Chapter 6.)

Directions

1 Paint the sides and edges of the hoop with gold paint. Set aside. Painting the hoop is optional, although it does look better if painted.

2 Print all the animals on the tracing vellum. The animals should face in the same direction. Print eight Carousel Poles, four Jester Sconces, and four Cherub Sconces also on the tracing vellum. Color each print on the printed side.

3 Cover the colored side of the prints with adhesive vinyl. Set the pole and sconce prints aside.

4 Cut out the animal prints by cutting on the edge of the print at the top and bottom (above and below the saddle). Then cut close to, but not on, the outer edges of the sides of each animal print. (Those areas will be recut in step 7.)

5 Turn the animal prints over, vinyl side down. Color this side of the print if desired. (It's necessary to color both sides of the print only if the colors from the right side are not visible on the wrong side.) Then lay a 12″ piece of clear nylon thread or fishing line in the center of the back of each print. Place one end of the thread or line at the lower edge of the print. The excess will extend beyond the top of the print.

6 Place a piece of adhesive vinyl over the entire back of each print. Make sure the thread is laying flat on the center of the print before covering it with the vinyl (Fig. 3-20).

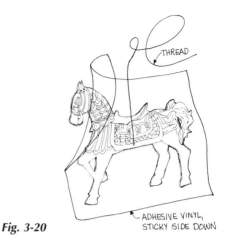

THREAD

ADHESIVE VINYL, STICKY SIDE DOWN

Fig. 3-20

7 Now cut out each print on the outer edges. Don't clip off the thread or line. Set all aside.

8 Place four markings on the top of the hoop so that it is divided into four equal sections.

9 Attach the mounting film (or double-faced tape) around the outer side of the hoop. Remove the paper covering from the film or tape.

10 Cut four 12″-long pieces of nylon thread or fishing line. Wrap the end of each piece of thread three times around the hoop at the markings. Wrap from the inner side to the outer side of the hoop. Stick the thread or line securely on the film (or tape). The other end of the threads will extend at least 10″ beyond the top of the hoop.

11 Mark the top of the hoop between each of the four pieces of thread. The hoop is now divided into eight sections.

12 Take one animal and wrap the thread extending from it three times around one of the marks you made in step 11. Begin wrapping on the outer side of hoop and end on the inner side. Attach the other seven animals in the same way.

13 Attach the decorative ribbon to the mounting film or tape on the outer side of the hoop. Set the hoop aside.

14 Cut out the pole prints. The cutting line should be close to (but not on) the edges of the print.

15 Lay the hoop with the animals on a flat surface. Lay a pole on top of the thread attached to an animal. The pole should be at least ½″ above the saddle of the animal. Attach the pole to the thread with removable tape. Attach the remaining seven poles on an animal thread in the same way.

16 When all poles are in place, hold the mobile up by its four threads (see step 10) to check the position of each pole. Rearrange the poles if necessary.

17 Place the mobile back on the flat surface. Cut eight ½″ × 5″ pieces of adhesive vinyl. Remove the cov-

ering on the vinyl. Turn the poles over, thread side up. Carefully remove the tape from the back of a pole print. Place a piece of vinyl on the back of the print, securing the thread in position. Repeat for the remaining seven poles.

18 Cut away the excess vinyl from the outer edges of the poles (and for goodness sake, don't clip off the threads!). Set the hoop aside.

19 Cover the back of the eight sconce prints with adhesive vinyl. Cut vinyl along the outer edges of the sconce. Attach a ½″ × ½″ piece of mounting film (or double-faced tape) on the hoop above each animal. The tape will be on the ribbon. Attach a sconce to the tape on the hoop, alternating the designs.

20 Twist together the four thread or line ends coming from the top of the hoop. Thread them through the eye on the snap swivel.

21 Holding the ends together, slide the French crimp over the ends and the four threads. This will form a loop around the eye of the swivel. Pinch the crimp closed with the needle-nosed pliers (Fig. 3-21).

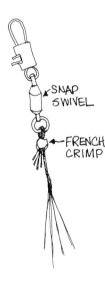

Fig. 3-21

22 It's done. Don't feel guilty if you decide to keep it.

Variations and Suggestions for Mobile Stamps

◗ If you don't want to make a mobile, use these stamps for a wall piece. Print and cut out the animals, poles, and sconces. Cover colored prints with adhesive vinyl. Use spacers (see Chapter 6) behind the animals for dimension. The pieces can be mounted on bristol board or foam core. The background can be decorated with prints or interesting papers (gift wrapping papers, origami, etc.) before attaching the prints.

◗ Print the animals on bristol board or foam core to use as a wall piece (no cutting or taping).

◗ Printing these stamps on fabric (shirts, bedding, pillows) offers endless options.

◗ Children would love using these stamps in a stamp book. They'd also enjoy making a mural on shelf paper with them.

Mail Art

One of the more interesting forms of paper stamping is mail art. "Stamp Pals" (as opposed to Pen Pals) is probably the best way to describe those who are involved. Mail art is done on a card (no envelope) that qualifies for postcard postage—minimum size is 3½″ × 5″; maximum size is 4½″ × 6″. The card must have at least one stamped print. What you do or say on the card is up to you.

If you'd like to be a part of this activity, subscribe to one (or all) of the stamping magazines listed in the Bibliography. They include names and addresses of fans of mail art as a regular feature.

Rebuses

Don't overlook the fun of sending a rebus to friends (and foes). *The Rebus Quarterly*, in addition to informative articles, lists names and addresses of rebus and Mail Art enthusiasts (see Bibliography).

EMBOSSED PAPER

☛ *Note:* Read "Pressure Embossing on Paper" in Chapter 6 before beginning.

Framed Quilt

The embossed and stamped quilt shown in the color section can be done very quickly. It's one of those won-

derful gifts that costs little to make and is so appreciated.

Supplies

Plastic quilt stencil from American Traditional Stencils

Pelle's See-Thru Stamps: Sunbonnet Sue; Sunbonnet Bill; Heart Block

One 9″ × 12″ sheet bristol paper (100-pound weight)

Embossing tool (or a dry ballpoint pen)

Pink and blue markers (or pastel chalk pencils or oil pastel sticks)

Pink and blue small cube-size pigment-ink pads (one each)

Light table or window

Removable tape

9″ × 12″ frame (optional)

Directions for Embossing

1 Attach the stencil securely to the right side of the paper, stencil up (Fig. 3-22).

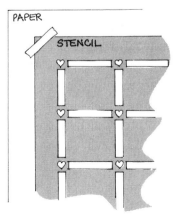

Fig. 3-22

2 Using pink and blue markers, color the borders and corner design of the stencil. Allow to dry.

3 Leave the stencil in place on the paper. Place the paper on the light table or attach to a window; paper is up.

4 Run the embossing tool around the edges of the stencil. Be sure you've embossed all of the design; run your fingers over the paper to feel the depression made with the embossing tool.

5 Remove the paper from the light table or window. Turn over and remove the stencil.

Directions for Printing

1 Decide how you want to arrange the quilt blocks in the open portions of the stencil.

2 Using the pink pigment-ink pad, print the Sunbonnet Sue. Using the blue pigment-ink pad, print the Sunbonnet Bill.

3 Using the pink pigment-ink pad, ink the Heart stamp. Cover the line around the block with tape (see "Masking" in Chapter 6). The tape will cover the line, and it will not print (Fig. 3-23). Print. Repeat this method of masking for each print. Allow the prints to dry.

Fig. 3-23

4 Sign and date the quilt. Place in the frame (matting optional).

Note Cards

Every bride needs thank you notes. Print her monogram within a pressure embossed design for an appreciated (and needed) gift. Remember to frame one for her to have as a keepsake.

Supplies

Alphabet stamps needed for monogram

Stencil from American Traditional with open area suitable for printing monogram (Fig. 3-24 is one example, © Judith Barker and American Traditional).

Gold pigment-ink pad (or color of your choice)

Blank note cards

Embossing tool

Light table or window

Fig. 3-24

Removable tape or marker glue for holding stencil in place

☞ ***Note:*** Read about pressure embossing in Chapter 6 before beginning.

Directions for Printing

1 Open the note card flat.

2 Secure the stencil to the front of the note card.

3 Stamp initials for the monogram in the center of the stencil opening. Allow the ink to dry.

☞ ***Note:*** Coloring portions of the stencil design is optional.

Directions for Embossing

1 Place the note card, front down, on the light table, or attach it to a window.

2 Run the embossing tool around the edges of the stencil design.

3 Lift the stencil from the note card.

Other Suggestions for Combining Stamps and Stencils

▶ Lamp shade kits with a cutting pattern for the shade are available. A paper lamp shade is perfect for combining embossed designs with stamp prints.

▶ Using tinted Jo Sonja's Texture Paste (see "Stamping on Wood" in Chapter 5) as paint, stencil a border design on a smooth plastered wall. Add coordinating stamp prints. Apply a clear protective finish when the Texture Paste and ink is dry. (Try a floral stencil with butterfly prints.)

CHILDREN'S PROJECTS

In addition to the Variations and Suggestions mentioned earlier, the following projects are suitable for children (and adults).

Before selecting products for children's use, read the label. Select only products labeled "suitable for use by children." And remember, solvent-based products, thermal embossing powders, heat guns, craft knives, and rotary cutters should not be used by children.

Birthday Fun for One and All

Supplies

☞ ***Note:*** Read about Sun Catchers in "Making Your Own Stamps" in Appendix A.

Delafield Stamp Company: Birthday Invitation

Sun Catchers (one for each child at the party)

Blocks for Sun Catchers (see step 2)

Glue or mounting film for blocks (Double-faced tape can be substituted but will not hold as well.)

Blank note cards for invitations

Tempera or poster paint

Dry foam pads or round cosmetic sponges (see step 7)

Freezer paper

Shelf paper or newsprint

Scissors or rotary cutter

White paper napkins

Plastic garbage bags and string

Small plastic bags

For the party: blunt-end scissors; marker glue; paper punches (optional); colored pencils, crayons, markers (optional); glitter and sequins (optional)

Before the Party

1 Print and send out the invitations.

2 Apply the blocks to the Sun Catchers. If the group is into sharing, one suction cup can be used on several stamps. Solid blocks can be mounted to stamps with glue or mounting film.

3 Bond freezer paper to freezer paper (shiny side to shiny side) and cut 15″ × 18″ rectangles to use as place mats.

4 Cut shelf paper into pieces that will be used for the stamp books (18″ × 12″ will be 9″ × 12″ when folded). Layer three or four of the cut edges in a pile, outer edges even. Apply the marker glue down the center of the back of one page and stick that page down on top of another page. Or you could machine stitch a long basting stitch down the center of the pile (if you have the time and inclination).

5 Make a "printer's apron" for each child from plastic garbage bags. Don't put them on the children until the printing begins.

☛ *Note:* For small children, poke a teeny hole on either side of the bottom of the bag. Reinforce the hole with tape. Thread a piece of string inside the bag from one hole over to the other hole. When you put the apron on the child, tie the string ends at the back of the child's neck. Tie a piece of string over the bag, around the child's waist.

For larger children, cut a 10″ slit at the bottom of the bag for the head to poke through. Cut a 4″ slit on each side for the arms to poke through. If the apron is flopping all over the place, tie a string around the child's waist to hold it down (the bag, not the child).

6 Cover the table with freezer paper, shiny side down. Tape widths together for large tables. If you'd rather use newsprint, cut plastic garbage bags apart and cover the table with those first. Put some strips of double-faced tape here and there on the plastic. The newsprint will stick to the tape and won't slide off the plastic. (Newsprint can also be used for the stamp books.)

7 If using round cosmetic sponges for ink pads, put a piece of double-faced tape on the back of the pads. Stick each one on either a yogurt container top, jar lid, cut-out pieces of plastic food wrap, or small plastic meat tray.

8 Ink the pads with poster or tempera paint just before the guests arrive. Place them in plastic bags and store in the refrigerator until needed.

Party Time

After the guests have had their fill of running and jumping and screaming, and all the presents are opened, settle everyone down at the table for a stamp fest. Have them decorate the table covering (the freezer paper or newsprint) first. After that's filled with prints, let them go to work on the place mats and napkins.

Now it's time to do the stamp books. Printing can be done directly on the pages of the book, or prints can be made on the cut sheets of shelf paper or newsprint and then colored, cut out, and glued to the pages of the book. All children love to use paper punches. But first decide if you want those little bits of paper flying all over the place.

Depending upon the age of the children, glitter can be sprinkled over marker glue that's wiped across the paper. If the children are between the ages of five and eight, keep an eye on the glitter. There's always one child who thinks it's colored sugar. Forget the glitter if anyone is under the age of 5. (Gick Glitter is certified nontoxic and safe for children to use, but that doesn't include eating.)

After everyone has stamped everything in sight (including the child sitting on the left), bring out the cake and ice cream. And I hope you have better luck with your cake than I had with mine. (Read about my disaster in "Frosting" in Chapter 5.)

Hope that the mothers will get there on time to pick up the guests. Send everyone out the door with their stamp book and a Sun Catcher stamp (Fig. 3-25).

Fig. 3-25

Sun Catchers can be used to print on fabric, too (see Chapter 4). If the children are eight and older, you may want to have a T-shirt printing party instead of a book printing party.

Stamp Books

Several stamp companies have blank books for children to use for stamped stories. The books are included with a set of stamps pertaining to a specific theme (everything from dinosaurs to the Wizard of Oz to Winnie the Pooh). Or you can pick up a couple of sketch books at a crafts or art supply store.

Sketch books range in size from 3″ × 5″ to 11″ × 17″. They're a good inexpensive blank book to use for stamping a story, practicing spelling, making funny faces, learning counting, and any other stamping activity imaginable. The type with a spiral spine is easier to use because the pages lay flat.

Variations and Suggestions for Children's Projects

Dozens of fantastic alphabet stamps are available. And their use is not limited to children by any means. The Ranger Industries, Inc. set is easy to use. The dies are polymer and mounted on small, clear plastic boxes.

Children find all kinds of ways to use the Funny Features (Fig. 3-26, © Inkadinkado, Inc.). My grandson, Jack, printed some spectacular faces and drew the needed bodies with permanent markers on 8½″ × 11″ sheets of removable stickers. After cutting them out, he had a great collection of stickers to use on a wipe-off white board.

I don't think the Victorian Paper Doll Bears by Rubber Stampede should be limited to children. This is one of those toys I let the children use after I've had my

Fig. 3-26

Fig. 3-27

fun. Be sure to cover the paper doll prints with adhesive vinyl. That keeps the rips, tears, and tears down to a minimum.

Preschoolers can be encouraged to learn numbers when the number stamps are handy (Fig. 3-27, © Stuck on Stamps 1993). But don't keep the prints hidden between the pages of a stamp book. The front of a T-shirt is one place they should go. The complete set has numbers 1 through 10.

If your children are enthralled with *Dinotopia* by James Gurney, they're familiar with the alphabet and numbers shown in the book. The alphabet and numbers are combinations of the symbol used for the letter A. Carve that symbol in an eraser (see "Making Your Own Stamps" in Appendix A). The children can use the stamp for sending secret messages to friends.

4

☛ STAMPING ON FABRIC

Stamping on fabric opens up a new world of creative fun with few limitations. As long as the fabric isn't too furry or textured, you can stamp on it. In fact, fabric is the first surface I think of when I think of stamping.

TIPS FOR STAMPING ON FABRIC

There are general rules that apply whenever fabric is decorated (painted, glued, fused, printed, etc.). Following them produces satisfactory results.

▶ Wash, dry, and press the fabric before printing. Don't use detergents containing bleach or softeners. Don't use liquid or sheet softeners. If wrinkles are difficult to remove, spray the fabric with water before pressing; don't use spray starch or sizing. Muslin and denim should be washed at least twice before printing. After these fabrics are dry, sprinkle drops of water on them. If drops are absorbed immediately, the fabric is ready for printing.

▶ Be absolutely certain the ink is permanent if you plan to launder the fabric. Don't use acrylic, perma-press, or treated fabrics (those with stain retardant, for example) for projects that will be laundered, because inks wash right out. If fabric will not be laundered (wall hangings, for example), you can use just about any type of fabric and any type of ink, including glass stain and glass paint.

▶ Stamps and inks do not produce the same result on every fabric. Always do test prints, especially on sweatshirt fleece and denim. The thickness and density of these fabrics may affect the results. For satisfactory printing on denim, opaque ink is usu-

ally required. Stop throwing out the legs when you turn jeans into cut/offs. And hang on to those old T-shirts and sweatshirts. Check out the remnant tables at the fabric store—grab the stuff that's reduced at half-price. For a few dollars, you can get all kinds of practice fabric.

▶ Bond freezer paper to the wrong side of fabric (see "Shirt Projects: Sweats and T's," below). Not only does the freezer paper serve as a "shirt board" to keep ink from soaking through fabric, but it also holds the fabric taut so that it's easier to color with a marker. Leave the freezer paper in place until after the paint and markers have been heat set. A Stamp-O-Round (see Positioning Tools, Chapter 6) holds fabric stable for printing and coloring. If this positioning tool is used, freezer paper is not necessary.

▶ If you prefer using an easel when you're coloring prints, slide a piece of cardboard, foam core, or a shirt board under yardage or inside shirts after the freezer paper has been bonded to the fabric. Secure the fabric to the easel with pins.

▶ Heat set fabric inks, including markers, unless label directions state not to. Press on the wrong side of the fabric, except when the directions on the label say to press on the right side. Usually ink should dry at least twenty-four hours before heat setting, but consult the label. Cover the fabric with cooking parchment paper when the required heat (normally a cotton setting) is higher than what is recommended for the fabric (Fig. 4-1). When using silk and synthetic fabrics, pretest in an inconspicuous spot. A heat gun used for embossing powder can also be used to heat-set paints. Hold the gun at

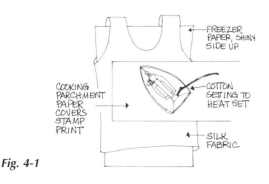

Fig. 4-1

Fig. 4-3

least 4″ from the fabric to avoid scorching the fabric.

Getting Started

Many techniques in Chapter 6 can be substituted for those described below. When substituting, remember to pretest. I didn't think you needed to be told when an iron and board were necessary—I know you *always* read the directions for a project before beginning.

SHIRT PROJECTS: SWEATS AND T'S

To mark the center front of a shirt, heat an iron to the cotton setting. Place the shirt on an ironing board, back side up. Fold the shirt in half, sleeves together. Press fold line on the shirt front (Fig. 4-2). The pressed line is the center front.

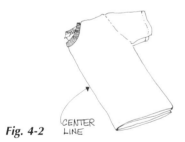

Fig. 4-2

To bond freezer paper to a shirt, heat an iron to the synthetic setting. Turn the shirt wrong side out. Cut a piece of freezer paper as wide and as long as the shirt (front or back). Place the shiny side of the freezer paper on the wrong side of the shirt. Press on the paper side of the freezer paper. Turn the shirt right side out when cool.

Talking Heads

If you like both farm animals and quilts, this shirt is for you. The heads can be printed on adhesive vinyl for earrings and necklaces (see "Shrink Plastic" in Chapter 5). Children have a great time coming up with head and shirt combinations (Fig. 4-3).

Supplies

Pelle's See-Thru Stamps: Shirts With Quilt Block Patterns (three quilt block patterns); Animal Heads (turkey, pig, goat, sheep, horse, rooster)

Pad or substitute with permanent ink

Shirt

Markers (optional)

Antifusant (see Appendix F)

Freezer paper

Ruler (wide quilting ruler)

Removable fabric marker

Directions

1 Press the center fold line of the shirt front. Bond freezer paper to the wrong side of the shirt front. Turn the shirt right side out.

2 Use a removable fabric marker to mark the center front. The line should extend at least 8″ down from the bottom of the neck ribbing.

3 Make parallel lines down the front of the shirt 3″ on either side of the center front line.

4 Make a line across the center front line, 3½″ down from the bottom of the neck ribbing, perpendicular to the center front line. Use a wide quilting ruler if you have one. Line up the ruler's vertical markings on the center front line.

5 Make a line 3½″ down from the line made in step 4.

6 Hold up the shirt. The three lines extending down the front of the shirt should be perpendicular to the neck ribbing. The two lines across the shirt front should be parallel to the neck ribbing.

7 To print the animals' shirts, position the stamp so that the buttons on the animal's shirt are on a line perpendicular to the neck ribbing and the bottom of the animal's shirt is on a line parallel to the neck ribbing.

8 To print the animals' heads, position the neck of the animal so that it is just inside the collar of the shirt. If necessary, use a fine-line permanent marker to extend the animal's neck into the collar.

9 Allow the prints to dry. Wipe out removable fabric marker, following the manufacturer's directions. Heat set the prints. Leave the freezer paper in place if the prints are colored.

10 If the prints are colored, apply antifusant and let dry. Color the prints with permanent markers.

11 Heat set the markers. Remove the freezer paper.

Good Grief, Joyce, What's That?

I love the Lady Tourist stamp. And the Whirly-wig is one of those go-anywhere, do-anything stamps (Fig. 4-4, © Quarter Moon Rubber Stamps). Check out the Beadery display in a craft's store to find acrylic mirrors or jewels to glue to the center of the Whirly-wig.

Fig. 4-4

Either stamp looks great thermal embossed on paper. The Tourist is a good stamp to use for a bookmark. Print the Whirly-wig in clay and use as a pin. Or print it on canvas shoes, using a metallic fabric paint as the ink.

Supplies

Quarter Moon Rubber Stamps: Lady Tourist; Whirly-wig

Shirt

Pad with permanent ink

Removable fabric marker

Permanent fabric markers to color Tourist prints

Antifusant

Glitter fabric paint for Whirly-wig

Acrylic mirrors or jewels to fit inner circle of Whirly-wig (optional)

Glue for acrylic mirrors or jewels

Directions

1 Press the center fold line down the shirt front. Bond freezer paper to the wrong side of the shirt front. Turn the shirt right side out.

2 Mark the center fold line with removable fabric marker. Mark a line across the center fold line, 5″ below neck ribbing.

3 To print the Tourists, center a Tourist on the middle line of the shirt front. Print a Tourist to the right and to the left ¼″ from the center print. The shoes of the Tourist prints are on the line marked across the center front line (Fig. 4-5).

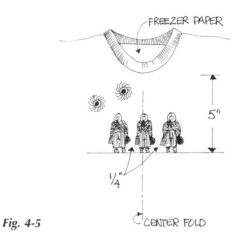

Fig. 4-5

4 To print the Whirly-wigs, print five or six randomly across the top of the shirt front, extending them up to one shoulder seam. The Whirly-wigs should be above the Tourist's hats.

5 Allow the prints to dry; heat set.

6 Apply antifusant to the shirt front. Allow to dry.

7 Color the Tourist prints with permanent fabric markers.

8 Apply glitter paint to the spokes of the Whirly-wigs. Dry flat. Apply glitter paint or glue to the center of the Whirly-wigs. Put an acrylic mirror or jewel into the paint or glue. The paint or glue should ooze slightly around edges of the mirror or jewel. Dry flat for at least four hours. Remove the freezer paper.

9 Do not launder for two weeks.

Wonderful Ladies (and a Couple of Men)

If you're a fan of elinor peace bailey and her wonderful family of dolls, you'll never take off this shirt (Fig. 4-6). If you haven't seen these creations before, be sure to look at her book *Mother Plays With Dolls* (see Bibliography).

Fig. 4-6

Any doll could be printed in clay and used as a pin. They'd be great on pillow covers. And you must admit that you know most of these characters in real life. Sending them a card printed with their special stamp belongs on your list of things to do (or ways to get even).

Supplies

Pelle's See-Thru Stamps: elinor peace bailey Dolls (twelve stamps are in the collection)

T-shirt

Scrap paper

6″-wide strip of freezer paper, as long as needed to go around bottom of shirt

Removable fabric marker

Pad with permanent ink (gold looks great)

Permanent markers (those with a micro-tip; optional)

Antifusant (optional)

Clear tape

Directions

1 Turn the shirt inside out. Press the freezer paper strip along the bottom edge of the shirt. Turn the shirt right side out.

2 Print all the stamps on scrap paper. Cut them out close to, but not on, the outer edges. Stick a small piece of tape on the top edge of each print. Number the front of each print.

3 Arrange the cut-out prints on the shirt back, just above the hem. (The tape will hold the prints in place.) Prints should be evenly spaced. On the shirt, use a removable marker to make a mark on both sides of the lower edge of each print. After removing each print, write the number of that print between the two marks with the removable fabric marker.

4 Arrange the cut-out prints on the shirt front, just above the hem. Place a mark on either side of the lower edge of each print. Leave the prints in place.

5 Print the stamps on the shirt back, just above the hem stitched, within the mark made in step 3. Use the number on each print as a guide for correct placement.

6 Remove the cut-out prints from the shirt front. Print the stamps on the shirt front as for the shirt back.

7 Optional: Apply a 3″-wide band of antifusant above the back hem. Allow to dry. Apply a 3″-wide band of antifusant above the front hem. Allow to dry.

8 Color the prints on the shirt back with permanent markers. Allow to dry. Color the prints on the shirt front. When all the prints are dry, heat set. Remove the freezer paper.

9 Rinse antifusant from the shirt following directions on the bottle.

☛ *Note:* Prints can be added to the sleeves, just above the hem, if desired. Follow the same procedure as above.

Puffy Teddy

This teddy is not in the center of the shirt front (Fig. 4-7). But if you think that would be a better place for it,

Fig. 4-7

by all means put it there. A shirt with three teddies sitting in a row would look good, too. Print the center teddy first; mask that print before printing another teddy on each side. Be sure the center print is dry before covering it with the mask. This stamp is also large enough to use with shrink plastic. A bracelet made from several plastic prints would be any little girl's joy, although maybe she'd prefer bed sheets with teddy prints. (Do both.)

Supplies

Comotion Rubber Stamp, Inc.: Jumbo Bear with Bow

Shirt

Freezer paper

Removable fabric marker

Puff paint, color of your choice (a white bear on a pink shirt is a good combination)

Rubber roller (brayer)

Wipe-Out Tool or cotton swabs

Iron or heat gun for puffing paint

Directions

1 Turn the shirt inside out. Press freezer paper to lower right side of shirt front. Turn the shirt right side out when cool.

2 With a removable marker, draw a line 3″ up from the bottom ribbing. Draw a line 4″ from the side seam (toward the center of the shirt front). These are the lines marking the placement of the print. Put the shirt on to check the placement. Remark lines if necessary.

3 Roll puff paint out on the freezer paper. The roller should be evenly coated with paint.

4 Roll the paint over the stamp. Remove excess ink from the block with the Wipe-Out Tool or cotton swabs.

5 Print next to the marked lines.

6 Let the paint dry. When dry, puff the paint, using an iron or heat gun (following the manufacturer's directions).

7 When cool, remove the freezer paper. Do not launder the shirt for at least one week.

☛ **Note:** The bow on the bear can be colored with a marker after the paint has been puffed.

The Wearable Aquarium

One of the nicest things I ever did for myself was to become a guide at the Monterey Bay Aquarium. The three-month course we were required to take opened

the door to the glories of the sea for this gal from northern Michigan. I had no idea that spectacular combinations of yellows, purples, oranges, blues, greens, and reds were common attire for sea animals.

So use any colors you can dream up for the fish in this aquarium. Whatever you select will be tame compared to the real thing.

You could use transfer ink. After making the prints on paper, transfer them to the shirt. Or you could print on Dritz Mending Fabric and fuse the prints to the shirt (see "Fuse It" in Chapter 7). After fusing, add glitter or crystal fabric paint and transparent tint. If you don't feel like making a shirt, make something with shrink plastic using the Jumbo prints.

Supplies

Comotion Rubber Stamp Company: Jumbo Tropical Fish; Jumbo Tropical Sun Fish; Tropical Fish; Tropical Angel Fish

Shirt (try blue)

Pad or substitute with permanent ink

Freezer paper

Curved ruler, French curve, or large bowl

Removable fabric marker

Safety pins

Permanent fabric markers in assorted colors

Antifusant

Glitter or crystal fabric paint

Transparent tint (optional)

Directions

1 Put on the shirt. Use safety pins to outline areas where you don't want prints. One place to avoid is

the underarm area; you can guess what other places to avoid.

2 Turn the shirt wrong side out. Bond freezer paper to the wrong side of the shirt back and front. Turn the shirt right side out. Slide the shirt over the end of an ironing board. Press on the right side to re-bond any loose freezer paper.

3 Using the curved ruler (French curve or bowl) as a guide, make curved lines with the removable fabric marker about 2″ up from bottom on the shirt back. It's supposed to look kind-of-like a wave (kind-of-like, not really like). Make another wavy line about 4″ above the first line.

4 Turn the shirt over. Make wavy lines on the shirt back as you did on the front. Connect the front and back lines. Make a third wavy line across the front about 3″ above the second line. Be sure to avoid areas marked with the safety pins. Hold the shirt up and check the arrangement of the lines. Change any you don't like.

5 There are two ways you can print the fish. Masks can be used with either method. The first method is just to go for it—put the prints anywhere you want (except over the safety pins). The second method takes a little more time. Make two or three prints of each fish on scrap paper. Cut out the prints close to, but not on, the outer edges. Stick a piece of tape on the top edge of each print. Arrange the cut-out prints on the shirt. (The tape will hold the prints in place.) When you like the arrangement, mark lightly around the prints with the removable marker. Remove the cut-out prints. Print on each marking.

6 Remove the safety pins. Heat set the prints. Apply antifusant; let dry.

7 Now comes the fun part—color each print to your heart's content. Allow to dry.

8 Use the tip of the glitter or crystal fabric paint bottle to paint the wavy lines on the shirt back. The bottle tip should drag along the fabric. Apply paint lines over the fishes that are on the waves. Make bubbles coming from the fishes' mouths with crystal fabric paint. (One small squeeze on the bottle is one bubble.) Dry flat. Apply paint to the shirt front in the same way. Dry flat.

9 Brush a light coat of transparent tint (either a blue or crystal tint) randomly over the shirt back. Dry flat. Brush tint randomly on the shirt front. Dry flat. Note: Each fish can be painted in a different color of transparent tint.

10 Do not launder the shirt for two weeks. If you go to the Monterey Bay Aquarium, be sure to wear this shirt (and tell those beautiful sea animals I miss them).

SILK PROJECTS

If you've never printed or painted on silk, it's time to start. Silk is as easy to print on as is paper. You can buy inexpensive blank silk scarves and hankies that are already hemmed. As soon as the prints are dry and heat set, the scarf or hanky is ready to use. A silk tie you've printed is the ideal gift for any man. Blank ties are available in both white and black.

If I haven't convinced you that working with silk is a piece of cake, use cotton. (See "Blank Clothing, Accessories, Yardage, Appendix F.")

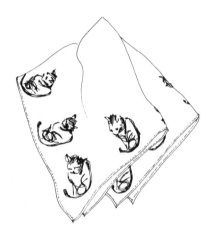

Speedy Scarf

This is a quickie. It takes less than thirty minutes from start to finish. If you'd rather spend less time than that, putting one print in the corner of a cotton hankie is an instant project. A silk T-shirt printed with this stamp would become a blouse any of us would be proud to wear. (This also is a good print for the upper corner of your stationery.)

I know there are a lot of steps. It'll take longer to read the instructions than it will to print the scarf.

Supplies

Mail Order Marking: Cat

Blank white silk scarf

Foam pad (or substitute) inked with Jacquard Metallic Black (or brand and color of your choice)

White gift wrap tissue paper (plain, without coating or design)

Freezer paper

Cooking parchment paper

Permanent marker, black

Removable clear tape

Directions

1 Wash the scarf in lukewarm water with mild soap. Press smooth between two sheets of cooking parchment paper.

2 Press the tissue paper smooth, using a synthetic setting on the iron.

3 Lay one piece of the tissue paper on a flat surface. Place the scarf on the tissue paper. The paper should extend at least 2″ beyond the outer edges of the scarf.

4 Stick one small piece of removable tape across each corner of the scarf, attaching it to the tissue paper. Additional strips of tape can be added to the long sides of the scarf if it's not stable on the tissue paper.

5 Use the permanent marker to draw the outline of the scarf on the tissue paper. Be careful not to get the marker on the scarf.

6 Lift the scarf from the tissue paper. The tissue paper will be used as a pattern for printing on the scarf. Do all of the printing on this tissue paper within the drawn lines.

7 Ink the stamp. Print a Cat in each corner of the tissue paper. It looks best if the Cat's head is toward the center of the scarf. Print a Cat in the middle of both long sides. Then print Cats between the middle Cats and the ones in the corners. Print Cats on the short sides. Allow the ink to dry.

8 Look at your design. If you think you'd like a different arrangement, make the outline of the scarf on another piece of tissue paper, as was done in steps 5 and 6. Repeat step 7.

9 Place a piece of clean tissue paper on freezer paper. Both papers should be at least 4″ wider and longer than the scarf. Tape the papers to your work surface. Tape the printed tissue paper to the top of the plain tissue paper, pattern side up.

10 Place the scarf on the printed tissue paper pattern. The edges of the scarf should be lined up with the drawn edges of the pattern made in step 5. Tape the scarf to the tissue paper pattern. Do not place tape over the areas that will be printed.

11 Print the scarf. The prints on the tissue paper pattern will be visible through the scarf. Use them as a guide when printing.

12 Remove the scarf from the tissue paper when the ink is dry. Heat set following the manufacturer's directions. Then go show off your scarf.

The Sensational, Spectacular Sun Print Scarf #1

Here's what you've been waiting for—the sun print technique. Plan ahead if you live in an area where sunlight is scarce in the wintertime. Or plan a trip to a tanning salon. Imagine the look on the owner's face when you walk in with your basket of scarves, stamps, and ink pads.

© Quarter Moon Rubber Stamps

Although these instructions are for a scarf (Fig. 4-8), you can also try this technique on ties. A knockout Christmas gift is a silk or cotton pocket hanky.

Fig. 4-8

Supplies

Paint Blocks: Large Flower

Blank white silk scarf (or cotton scarf)

Two Petifours or cosmetic sponge wedges

Setacolor Transparent Fabric Paint, emerald and yellow (or colors of your choice)

White gift wrap tissue paper (plain white with no coatings or prints)

Freezer paper

Scrap paper

Cooking parchment paper

Directions

1 Wash the scarf in lukewarm water, using a mild soap. Dry. Press smooth between two sheets of cooking parchment paper.

2 Dilute the fabric paint with water as directed on the paint container. Mix well.

3 Cover your work surface with two layers of freezer paper, shiny side up.

4 Cover the two layers of freezer paper with four layers of white tissue paper. The papers should be wider and longer than the scarf. Smooth the papers flat.

5 Place the scarf on the tissue paper. Smooth flat.

6 Ink one Petifour or wedge with yellow paint. Pat the ink on the stamp.

7 Cover the entire surface of the scarf with prints. The prints should overlap. Ink the stamp for each print. Rinse the ink from the Petifour or wedge with clear water (no soap) after all the printing is completed.

8 Leave the scarf on the tissue paper until the ink is dry (at least one hour). Throw out the tissue paper.

9 Wipe off any paint residue from the freezer paper. Cover it with four fresh layers of white tissue paper.

10 Make several prints (at least six) of the Flower on scrap paper. Any type of ink can be used for this printing. Cut out the prints along the outer edges.

11 Dip the scarf in warm water. Roll it in a towel to remove excess moisture. (Some of the prints may run.) Place the scarf on the tissue paper, printed side up.

12 Ink the second Petifour or wedge with the emerald paint. Pat the ink on the stamp. Print approximately twelve prints on the scarf. The prints should be spaced at least $1/2''$ apart.

13 When printing is completed, pick up the freezer paper by each end and take the scarf outside to soak up the sun. Place the cut-out masks made in step 10 randomly on the scarf. Wherever there's a mask, the ink will be lighter (see Scarf #2, step 13, below, for a windy-day solution).

14 Rinse the ink from the Petifour or wedge.

15 Leave the scarf in the sun for at least one hour. Remove the scarf from the tissue paper. Put the scarf between two pieces of cooking parchment

paper. Heat set according to the manufacturer's directions. You'll now be known as the best scarf printer in town.

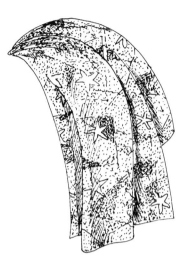

The Sensational, Spectacular Sun Print Scarf #2 (It's not easy thinking up names for all this stuff.)

Supplies

Stuck On Stamps: Background Print; Starfish (from Stamps of the Deep set)

Blank white silk scarf

Foam pad or substitute inked with Setacolor Opaque Fabric Paint, gold

Foam pad or substitute inked with Setacolor Transparent Fabric Paint, emerald

Foam pad or substitute inked with Setacolor Transparent Fabric Paint, blue

Cooking parchment paper

White gift wrap tissue paper (no coatings or prints)

Freezer paper

Directions

1 Wash the scarf in lukewarm water, using a mild soap. Press smooth between two pieces of cooking parchment paper.

2 Cut at least twelve $2''$ squares of freezer paper. Print the Starfish on the paper side of two of the squares. (Any type of ink can be used for these prints.)

3 Stack five of the cut freezer paper squares in a pile, with the edges somewhat even. Place one of the printed squares on top of the stack. Using that print as a pattern, cut out the Starfish through the

stack of freezer paper squares. Place the other printed square on top of the five remaining squares. Cut out the Starfish. You'll have a dozen star-shaped cut-out designs. Don't worry if there are a few stars that look a little odd.

4 Cut a piece of freezer paper that is longer and wider than the scarf. Place it on a flat work surface, shiny side up.

5 Ink a pad with the opaque paint. The pad should be evenly saturated with the paint.

6 Spread the scarf on the freezer paper. Smooth all the wrinkles flat.

7 Print the Starfish all over the scarf. The prints should not be touching. Leave the scarf flat on the freezer paper until the paint is thoroughly dry.

8 Dilute each color of the Transparent Fabric Paint, in separate containers, according to the manufacturer's directions. Stir well.

9 Ink one pad with the first color of Transparent Fabric Paint; ink another pad with the second color.

10 Ink the Background Print stamp with the first color of ink. Print the scarf. The prints should not completely cover the scarf. Clean the ink from the stamp with a damp sponge. Dry the die and block.

11 Ink the Background Print stamp with the second color of ink. Print any areas of the scarf not printed with the first color of ink. The second color will overlap and cover the first color in many areas of the scarf. When finished printing, place the stamp, die down, on a damp sponge. (Clean the ink from the stamp after taking the scarf outside.)

12 Pick up the freezer paper by the ends and take the scarf outside. Place the star masks made in step 3 on the scarf wherever they look good. Leave the scarf in the sun for at least one hour. If it's a windy day, those little stars will flit right off the scarf. To avoid that from happening, put a piece of cardboard under the freezer paper. Push a pin through the center of each star into the cardboard. The pins will hold the stars in place.

13 Remove the scarf from the freezer paper. Place the scarf between two layers of cooking parchment paper. Heat set according to the manufacturer's directions. Now you have two dynamite scarves.

USING STENCILS AND STAMPS TOGETHER

The Golden Eagle Jean Jacket

This stencil seems meant for these stamps, but it certainly isn't the only combination that is available. There are dozens of stencil and stamp combinations you can use.

Supplies

Mostly Animals: Majestic Eagle; Stylized Eagle

Pebeo Eagle Stencil (see Pebeo, Appendix E)

Denim jacket

Pebeo Puff Paste (Createx Puff and Pearl All-Surface Puff Binder are suitable substitutes)

Setacolor Gold opaque fabric paint (Createx Gold Textile Color or Pearl All Surface Gold are suitable substitutes)

Marker glue

Freezer paper

Piece of cardboard, foam core, or a shirt board, as wide and long as the back of the jacket

Straight pins

Plastic charge card or paint spreader

Wedge-shaped cosmetic sponge (or disposable foam brush)

Large safety pins

Rubber roller; plastic spoon

Heat source for puffing paint (see label)

Directions for Stenciling

☛ *Note:* If you haven't stenciled before, do a small practice piece before beginning the jacket. Place the stencil on scrap fabric and apply paint as directed in step 7. When the paint is dry, lift the stencil to check the results. It's not a bad idea to puff up the paint to check out the puff factor before beginning.

1 Wash and dry the jacket twice. Don't use any type of softener in the wash cycle or dryer. Sprinkle

drops of water on the jacket. If the drops are absorbed immediately, the jacket is ready to paint. If the drops are not absorbed, wash and dry the jacket again.

2 Apply a light coating of marker glue to the wrong side of the stencil. Dry for ten minutes or until the glue appears dull.

3 Press the freezer paper to the wrong side of the back of the jacket.

4 Place the stencil in the center of the jacket back. If the jacket has a yoke, place the stencil below the yoke. Check the position and angle of the stencil. Rearrange if desired. Using either a rubber roller or the back of a plastic spoon, push the stencil securely to the jacket.

5 Place the cardboard, foam core, or shirt board against the wrong side of the jacket back. Push straight pins through the jacket into the cardboard. The fabric should be taut but not stretched.

6 Mix Setacolor Gold with Pebeo Puff Paste according to the manufacturer's directions.

7 Place a spoonful (plastic spoon) of the paste/paint mix on the edge of the stencil, next to one of the cut openings. Use the charge card or paint spreader to pull the paint over the edge of the stencil onto the fabric. Don't pull the paint from the fabric to the edge of the stencil, which pushes the paint under the edge of the stencil (Fig. 4-9). Continue this process of adding paint along the edges of the stencil and pulling it onto the fabric until the outer edges of the stencil are painted. Add paint to the fabric in the center open area of the stencil. Spread paint evenly either with the card or spreader, or with the narrow end of a wedge-shaped cosmetic sponge.

Fig. 4-9

8 If you'd like more puff in some areas of the eagle, pat extra paint on those areas with the end of the wedge.

9 After the paint is thoroughly dry, remove the jacket from the cardboard. Don't puff the paint now. Do all the puffing after the stamp prints are dry.

Directions for Stamping

1 Put on the jacket. Use safety pins to mark where you want to place the eagle prints. Put two or three on the back yoke (or back shoulder area). Put one or two on the front yoke (or front shoulder area). Prints can be placed in any area without seam lines. (Stamps won't print evenly over the double-stitched seams in jean jackets.)

2 Put the jacket back on to check the placement of the pins; rearrange if necessary. (Each pin marks where a print will be placed.)

3 Roll the Puff Paste/Setacolor Gold mix out on freezer paper to coat the roller. The coating should be even.

4 Roll the ink (the paste/paint mix) over a die. Print the jacket back first. Don't push down too hard on the stamp when printing. You want as much ink as possible on the surface of the fabric. When all the printing on the back is completed, dry flat until the prints are thoroughly dry.

5 Print the jacket front, using the same procedure as used in step 4. Dry flat until the prints are thoroughly dry.

6 Apply heat, according to the manufacturer's directions, to puff the painted stencil design and prints.

QUICK PROJECTS

Pot Holders and Place Mats

When you need a gift in a hurry, nothing is faster than a pot holder. Cut two pieces of sweatshirt fabric in the desired size. Place them wrong sides together and stitch on the right side, ½″ from the cut edges. Place mats can be made in the same way. Be sure to read *Too Hot To Handle?* by Doris Hoover (see Bibliography). This book has dozens of ideas for pot holders.

Pillows

Use either a purchased pillow cover (see Pillow Covers and Pillow Forms in Appendix F) or make one. If using a ready-made pillow cover, slide a piece of cardboard or foam core inside the cover before printing. The cardboard provides the flat surface needed for clear prints. If making your own, print the fabric before stitching the seams. Large-size stamps can be used for a variety of speedy projects, such as blocks for quilt tops (Fig. 4-10 © Stamp.A.Quilt for Fabric 1994).

Use this stamp with the large heart shape to print an appliqué to fuse on a pillow cover. After applying the web to the wrong side of a piece of cotton calico fab-

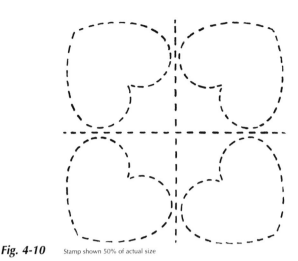

Fig. 4-10   Stamp shown 50% of actual size

ric, make one print on the right side of the fabric. Cut excess fabric ¼″ from the outer edges of the print. Cut out the heart shapes. Fuse the print to the center of the pillow cover for an instant decorated pillow. You could also add a fine line of fabric paint or machine satin stitch along the fused edges.

The Kokopelli designs by Great Notions Rubber Stamps look terrific on a pillow. Print the rounded grouping in the center of the cover. Then print the large single figure in each corner (see Fig. 5-12). Use the linear grouping to print a border between the large single prints. (Metallic copper or bronze fabric paint is a good choice for the ink.)

Bags and Totes

Mary Mulari's book *Travel Gear and Gifts to Make* has instructions for making a variety of bags and totes.

The barrel bag is the perfect size for a "train tote" for the wooden train described in "Stamping on Wood" in Chapter 5. Children love handles on their totes, so add a twill tape loop in one of the end seams of the bag. The loop should be large enough to fit easily over the hand of the child using the bag (Fig. 4-11).

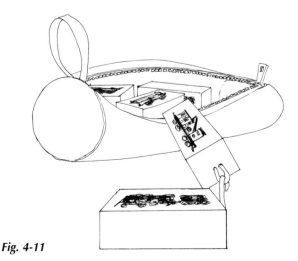

Fig. 4-11

Make two laundry bags as instructed in Mary's book. Use one for laundry. Use the other to take to the beach. Put the always-needed bottle of sunscreen in the pocket on the outside of the bag. The large sea shell stamp from Mail Order Marking is made to order for a beach bag (Fig. 4-12) (and the back of a beach coat).

Fig. 4-12

Ribbons

The long floral design below (Fig. 4-13, © 1994 Stamp Affair) is a great "ribbon printer." Mask one end of the die to print a continuous design the length of the ribbon.

Fig. 4-13

Print on satin ribbon for an inexpensive sash for a child's dress. Prints on satin hair ribbons would complete the outfit.

To create inexpensive, but fancy, ribbons and bows for gift wrapping, print the floral design on white polypropylene craft ribbon with gold pigment ink.

If none of these ideas sounds too exciting, how about adding prints around the collar of a shirt and embroidering them?

Bookmarks

About the only time we think of making fabric bookmarks is for cross-stitched patterns. It only takes one fast roll with a Rollagraph Stamp Wheel to print a bookmark. After printing, cover both sides of the fabric with adhesive vinyl. The vinyl should extend slightly beyond the edges of the fabric (Fig. 4-14).

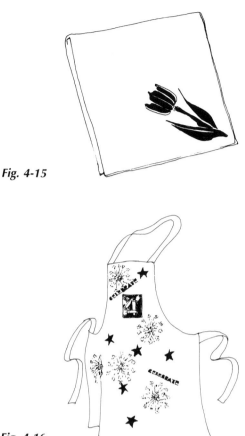

Fig. 4-15

Fig. 4-14

Pocket Hankies

These can be used for the nose, too, although I have to admit that there aren't too many of us left who prefer cloth to the paper variety. However the hankies are used, they're quick to print.

You can create a garden of prints with stamps from the Magna-Stamp P.O. Floral Collection. The prints can be placed in one corner, all four corners, or over the entire hanky (Fig. 4-15).

Apron

P.O. Box Rubberstamps has an assortment of stamps that take care of the cook's apron (Fig. 4-16), plus the napkins, paper cups, and invitations for a Fourth of July

Fig. 4-16

bash. You could even stamp a T-shirt for each guest. (Better yet, have them stamp their own.)

Ties and Belts

If you enjoy making neckties (from silk or other suitable fabrics), don't overlook the tie pattern from The Crowning Touch, Inc. (see Appendix E). It eliminates the hassles usually encountered when making ties. I think the Skier stamp from Graphistamp belongs on a tie, don't you (Fig. 4-17)? There's also the Golfer stamp—I'll let you decide which one to use.

Fig. 4-17

Fasturn tools (another product from The Crowning Touch) really do turn tubes quickly. They're available in about every size you could need. A few prints on fabric, a little stitching, a quick turn, and you've got an original belt. Usually the Tic Tac Toe stamp set from Stamp Affair is thought of as child's play. But you must admit that a belt made from three braided tubes, each with a different print from this set, would be quite an eye-catcher (Fig. 4-18).

Sun Catcher Prints

Sun Catchers (see Chapter 1; "Children's Projects" in Chapter 3; Appendix A) can be used to print on fabric (Fig. 4-19). Ink the stamp with either fabric paint in the dabber bottle or a foam pad (or substitute) inked with fabric paint. Coloring prints with fabric markers is optional, although children usually consider coloring a necessity rather than an option.

Almost every brand of fabric paint is nontoxic (check the label) and can be safely used by children. Fabric paint is permanent when dry, which is great when printing on fabric. It's not great if the paint is all over the walls and carpets. Clean up spills immediately.

Fig. 4-18

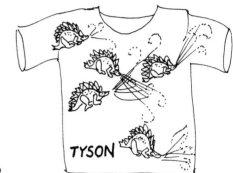

Fig. 4-19

5

WOOD, PLASTIC, CLAY, GOURDS, FROSTING, FUN FOAM, ROCKS, AND FACES

You've read that paper is the most popular surface for stamping and that the first surface I think of is fabric. But it doesn't end there. The surfaces included in this chapter are only a few of the many suitable for printing.

TIPS FOR STAMPING ON POROUS SURFACES

Read the label to ensure you have selected the correct ink, paint, or marker for the surface you have selected. Fabric paint in a dabber bottle (Fabra-ca-Dabra is one brand) is usually suitable as a permanent ink on porous surfaces such as wood, Fun Foam, etc. Be sure to pretest. Inking with a felt pad may not produce satisfactory results for printing on all of the surfaces included in this chapter. Again, pretest. Look through Chapter 6 for ideas on the many techniques that can be used on the surface included below.

STAMPING ON WOOD

Before beginning a project, lightly sand all the surfaces. Use emery boards if you don't have sandpaper; even the old, used ones work. Put a sealer on all sides and edges of the wood after sanding. Several products are suitable. Jo Sonja's All Purpose Sealer can be used as either a sealer or a protective finish on many surfaces in addition to wood; you can tint with Jo Sonja's Artist Colors. Gare Colorwash adds a slight color to wood, as does

Ceramcoat Transparent Wood Glaze by Delta. Dilute Plaid Stencil Paint for a wash effect. Dilute nondimensional fabric paints for a light tint. Ceramcoat Hi-Gloss Water Based Enamel by Delta and DecoArt Ultra Gloss Acrylic Enamel provide complete coverage, as do Accent Hobby Craft High Gloss Enamel and Accent Water Base Staining Glaze. Any of these products can also be used as ink.

Any wood item that will be handled (boxes, for example) should be given a protective finish after printing. Spraying is the best method of application if watercolor inks, markers, colored pencils, or oil pastel sticks are used for coloring prints.

Hard and Soft Woods

The first thing to do is to go to the lumberyard and check out the scrap box. There may be some pieces in there that are just what you want. If not, most lumberyards cut pieces to order. Good for printing are 1 × 2's, 2 × 2's, 2 × 4's, and 4 × 4's. All can be cut to the length you need. When you need a large chunk of wood, use a 6 × 6. For wider pieces, use cut pieces of shelving.

Balsa Wood

Balsa wood is a stamper's dream. It's inexpensive; it cuts easily with a rotary cutter, craft knife, or small craft saw; and it prints like a charm. You can buy it by the piece, but I like the assorted packs, which include a variety of sizes and thicknesses and are a better bargain than buying wood by the piece. If you can't find balsa wood locally, see Tower Hobbies in Appendix E.

Flower Basket

I jumped up and down after printing this stamp with Jo Sonja's Texture Paint. I couldn't believe how great the print turned out—it's really something to see (Fig. 5-1, © First Impression Rubber Stamp Arts).

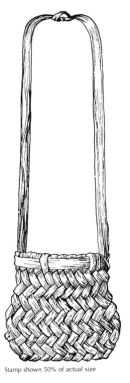

Fig. 5-1 Stamp shown 50% of actual size

Supplies

First Impression: Large Orchid Basket by Rainy Day Stamps

4″ × 10″ × ⅜″ (or thicker) piece of balsa wood

Sealer (clear or tinted)

Sandpaper or emery board

About 2 ounces of Jo Sonja's Texture Paste

Plastic teaspoon

Slight amount of Jo Sonja's Artist Color for tinting Texture Paste (optional)

Piece of freezer paper

Rubber roller (brayer)

Scrap paper

Cotton swabs or Wipe-Out Tool

Permanent glue

Small silk flowers and leaves

Small hanger for back of plaque

Directions

1 Sand the balsa wood smooth. Apply sealer to both sides and ends of the wood. Let dry.

2 Put a heaping teaspoon of Texture Paste in the center of a 12″-long piece of freezer paper. Add a dab of Artist Color (more can be added for a darker tint) to the paste. Blend together well with the back of the plastic spoon.

3 Roll paste/paint mixture (this will be the ink) out on freezer paper. The roller should be evenly coated with ink.

4 Roll ink over the die. Wipe off any ink that's on the cushion or block with a Wipe-Out Tool or a cotton swab.

5 Print on the scrap paper. If the detail of the basket isn't clear, there was too much ink on the roller. Continue making test prints until the print is clear.

6 Print the basket in the center of the plaque. Let dry thoroughly.

7 Create a floral arrangement with silk flowers and leaves on top of the basket. Give the appearance of some blossoms having fallen from the basket. Glue the arrangement in place (Fig. 5-2).

Fig. 5-2

8 Attach the hanger to the back of the plaque.

Variations and Suggestions for Flower Basket Stamp

- Use a puff fabric paint to ink the stamp (see Chapter 4; "Puff Paints" in Appendix B). Print on the front of a shirt. Stitch an arrangement of silk flowers and leaves in the basket.

- Print a basket on the fronts of cupboards using Texture Paste/Artist Color ink. Print flowers in each basket. Apply clear varnish over the prints for protection.

◆ Use the print on the fronts or backs of doors. Print a cascading floral arrangement in and around the basket. Use Texture Paste/Artist Color ink for the prints. Apply exterior varnish over the prints for protection.

◆ Print a border on a wall using Texture Paste/Artist Color ink. Apply a clear varnish over the prints for protection.

◆ Obviously this stamp can be printed on paper with either dye-based or pigment ink. It's beautiful on the front of a card.

Another Magnetic Idea (the first is in Chapter 3)

A magnet back on a balsa wood print is a low-cost gift that is always appreciated. For unique results, color with water-soluble colored pencils and pastel chalk pencils.

Supplies

Delafield Stamp Company: Country Scene

One piece of balsa wood, $4\frac{1}{2}'' \times 5\frac{1}{2}'' \times \frac{1}{8}''$

Craft knife or rotary cutter and cutting mat

Sandpaper or emery board

Sealer

One $4'' \times 5\frac{1}{2}''$ piece of Magnet Maker

Pad or substitute with permanent ink

Colored and/or pastel pencils (assorted colors)

Protective finish in spray canister

Directions

1 Cut the wood to the size of a stamp. Apply the sealer and let dry.

2 Print on the best side of the wood. Allow the ink to dry.

3 Color the print with colored and pastel pencils.

4 Spray protective finish over the print. Let dry thoroughly.

5 Remove the paper covering the adhesive side of the magnetic sheeting. Place the wood on the adhesive.

6 Trim the excess magnetic sheeting around the sides of the wood.

Variations and Suggestions for Magnetic Idea Stamp

◆ Using permanent ink, make four prints in the center of a pillow cover. Color the prints in a Winter, Spring, Summer, and Fall motif.

◆ Use the stamp for printing on postcards or blank note cards.

◆ Have children use this stamp as the basis for a story in a stamp book.

Bookends

I think prints belong on bookends. On the other hand, this is coming from someone who told you to use fabric to make bookmarks—and calls a Sun Catcher a stamp.

Use the same print for bookplates. The books with that print inside the cover go between the bookends with that same print. It's an easy way for children to keep their books in order.

Supplies

Mail Order Marking: Sailing Boat

Two unfinished wooden bookends (purchase at crafts store)

Sandpaper

Sealer

Small brush (disposable)

Pad or substitute with permanent ink

Permanent markers (optional)

Dritz Adhesive Felt

Protective finish (brush-on or spray type)

Directions

1 Sand all the sides smooth. Apply a thin coating of sealer to all the surfaces. Allow to dry.

2 Print on the front of the bookends (the sides that will be seen). Color the prints with markers.

3 Apply protective finish to all sides of each block. Allow to dry thoroughly.

4 Apply Dritz Adhesive Felt to the bottom of each bookend.

5 Use the stamp for printed bookplates. Write the owner's name in the open space at the bottom of the print (Fig. 5-3, © Mail Order Marking 1992).

DAVID GILLEN, JR.

Fig. 5-3

Variations and Suggestions for Bookends Stamp

◆ Make bookmarks for the books that have this print as their bookplate. Print on paper. Apply adhesive vinyl to the front and back of the print. Cut along the outer edges of the print.

The Greatest of All Wooden Trains

These train stamps are made from original drawings of Paya Toys, a world-renowned tin toy manufacturer in Spain. The Mail Order Marking catalog has information about the history of Paya Toys and a complete assortment of stamps from the drawings. They also sell the toys, which are collector's items. And the stamps allow children the opportunity to enjoy the designs.

I got so tired of broken wooden wheels (little feet have a way of trampling on everything) when my children were small. These train cars don't have wheels (Fig. 5-4). The train is a push toy in the clearest sense of the word. (You can, of course, add wheels.)

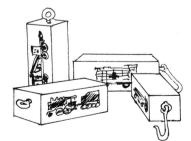

Fig. 5-4

Supplies

Mail Order Marking: Paya Train Engine and Coal Car; Paya Log Car; Paya Derrick; Paya Caboose

Four pieces of 2 × 4's (each piece should be ½" longer than the stamp for each car)

Four brass screw eyes; four brass hooks (size 10 or larger; not too small for little fingers to hook and unhook)

Sandpaper

Sealer

Pad or substitute with permanent ink

Protective finish (a heavy-duty one)

Scrap paper

Directions

1 Print train cars on scrap paper. Take the prints to the lumberyard and have a 2" × 4" cut for each car. The piece should be ½" longer than the car.

2 Sand and apply sealer to the wood pieces.

3 Print each train car on the top center of the piece of wood intended for that car. Allow the ink to dry.

4 Apply protective finish to all sides and ends of the wood pieces.

5 Attach one screw eye in the front end of each piece of wood. Attach a hook in the back end. Hand the train over to the engineer. (By the way, the hooks and eyes are about as good as anything a child can use to develop finger coordination.)

Variations and Suggestions for Train Stamps

◆ Heavy-duty hook-and-loop tape can be used instead of the hooks and eyes for the ends of the wood. Use the hook side on the front end and the loop side on the back end of the pieces.

◆ Mail Order Marking sells 18" × 1¼" × ¾" pieces of the finished wood used for the mounts for these stamps. The prints fit perfectly on the top of the wood. It can be left in one piece for a train that is 18" long. Or it can be cut into smaller pieces to fit each car. The grooves on the side of this wood are great for little fingers to hang on to.

◆ Make a "train tote" using the barrel bag pattern in Mary Mulari's book, *Travel Gear and Gifts to Make* (see Chapter 4).

◆ Use tinted Jo Sonja's Texture Paste as an ink for raised prints on wood or foam core that are used as wall decorations.

Valentine Cube

Everyone sends Valentine cards. I'm ready for a change—it's time we switched to Valentine cubes. If

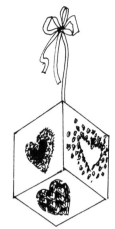

Fig. 5-5

you don't like the idea of a wooden cube, use a small paper box (Fig. 5-5).

Supplies

Graphistamp: Hearts (six stamps)

One 1½" length piece of 2 × 2 (A 2 × 2 isn't really 2 × 2, it's 1½" × 1½".); or 1½" wooden cube purchased in a crafts store

Sandpaper or emery board

Silver fabric paint, diluted (or color of your choice)

Pad or substitute with permanent red ink

Small brass screw eye (optional, used if cube is hung from ceiling)

⅛"-wide red satin ribbon 36" long (optional, used if cube is hung from ceiling)

Directions

1 Ask the lumberyard to cut a 1½" piece of 2 × 2. The piece should be as square as possible.

2 Sand the cube and paint it with diluted fabric paint. Allow to dry.

3 Print each side of the cube with a different heart.

4 Attach the screw eye in center of one side of the cube.

5 Attach the ribbon to the screw eye.

6 Place the cube in a small box and give it with love.

Variations and Suggestions for Valentine Cube Stamps

▶ If your children take their lunches to school, finding one of these prints in the lunch box would certainly add to their day. Use blank index cards cut into quarters for the paper.

▶ Some of these stamps could be used as appliqué patterns to include in your next heart quilt. If the thought of hand appliqué seems too tedious, stitch

on the machine. Use the blind stitch with invisible nylon thread.

▶ And if that seems too tedious, use as fused appliqués.

▶ Or just print them on stickers. (Do the quilt next year.)

STAMPING ON PLASTICS (HARD AND SOFT)

Either soft or hard plastic can be printed with stamps, although the surface of hard plastic has to be "roughed up" before printing. Use sandpaper or an emery board and a very light touch when sanding.

Soft plastics cannot be roughed up. Apply a suitable sealer (Jo Sonja's All Purpose Sealer, for example) before and after printing to protect the print.

Inks for Plastic

One problem encountered when printing on plastic is finding a low-cost surface to use for test prints. Plastic food wrap is not a guaranteed test surface, but it does let you know if an ink *won't* stick to plastic. What you can't tell is how permanent the stick will be. All of the inks mentioned here print well on plastic and are permanent. Be sure, however, to read the label before using an ink on plastic because recommended surfaces for a product sometimes change. If plastic is not listed on the label, select another ink.

Solvent-based inks specifically intended for shrink plastic are available from Comotion Rubber Stamps, Inc. and Ranger Industries, Inc. (see Appendix E). DecoArt Ultra Gloss Acrylic Enamel and DEKA Gloss Air can also be used on this plastic and can be baked. Follow the directions on the label.

Other craft paints that can be used successfully on hard and soft plastics are glass stain and glass paint. These paints are used for painting glass and plastic surfaces such as Sun Catchers. Select darker colors; transparent colors don't print well. Brands include Craft House, DEKA, Delta, Palmer, Pebeo, and Plaid.

Several brands of markers can be used on plastics. (Again, check the label.) Zig Posterman Markers and Sakura Identi-Pen are permanent on most soft and hard plastics. Testors Gloss Paint Markers can be used on hard plastics.

Aquarium Curtain

By now you know that I'm into fish. And what better place for fish than a shower curtain? This project isn't complicated. If preplanning bores you, just stamp away (Fig. 5-6).

Supplies

Mostly Animals: Rockfish; Scalefish; Spike Fish; Glasseye Fish; Large Pouting Mandarin; Small Pouting Mandarin; Soldier Fish; Aquarium Grass;

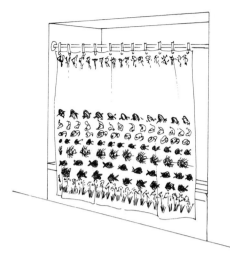

Fig. 5-6

Large Aquarium Plant; Small Aquarium Plant; Large Water Greenery

White plastic shower liner with a texture surface (I got one on sale for $1 at a discount store. Scout around—you may find a bargain.)

Shelf paper (cheapest brand available)

Masking or clear tape

Pebeo Water-based Glass Stain (Vitrail a L'Eau), several dark colors (substitute with brand of your choice)

Plastic food wrap

Wedge-shaped cosmetic sponges

Permanent markers suitable for plastic (optional)

Jo Sonja's All Purpose Sealer for sealer and finish coat (substitute with brand of your choice)

Small disposable foam paintbrush (or cosmetic wedge)

Pencil

Removable fabric marker

Scrap paper

Removable clear tape

Directions

1 Open the shower curtain. Let it hang a couple of days to get rid of the creases and folds, or press it with an iron on very low heat. (Cover the plastic with tissue paper or cooking parchment paper when pressing.)

2 Make at least two prints of each stamp on scrap paper. Cut out close to the outer edges of the design.

3 Cut shelf paper the same length as the curtain. Tape (masking or clear) pieces together so that the paper is as wide as the curtain. Lay on a flat surface.

4 Arrange cut-out prints on the shelf paper. Use removable tape to hold the prints in place while you're pondering the arrangement. When you're satisfied, trace around each print with a pencil. As you remove each print, write the name of the print inside the traced lines. You can also include the color of ink that will be used for that print. Do this for all the prints.

5 Pretest the removable marker on the shower curtain (in an inconspicuous spot). It should wipe off completely.

6 Put the shower curtain on a flat surface. Place the cut-out prints in position on the shower curtain, using the shelf paper with the traced prints as a guide. Use removable tape to hold the prints in place. Trace around the outer edges of the prints with the removable fabric marker. Remove the cut-out prints.

7 Brush a thin coat of the sealer within, not over, the lines drawn on the shower curtain. Allow to dry. Wipe off the tracings made with the removable marker.

8 Wipe a counter with a damp sponge. Spread a small piece of plastic food wrap on the damp counter. Smooth flat with the sponge.

9 Apply a gloop of glass stain (or glass paint) the size of a fifty-cent piece on the plastic food wrap. Dip the wide end of the cosmetic wedge into the stain. The end of the wedge should be saturated with the stain.

10 Ink a stamp with the color selected for that stamp (refer to shelf paper tracings). Print on the shower curtain. The prints should be on top of the sealer. Repeat this for all the colors. Allow to dry.

11 Color the prints with permanent markers if desired.

12 When ink and markers are dry, brush a thin coat of the sealer over each print. The sealer should extend slightly beyond the edges of the print. Now that's a shower curtain!

Variations and Suggestions for Aquarium Curtain Stamps

▶ Print some, or all, of the stamps on the bathroom window curtain. (Use permanent fabric ink if the curtain is fabric.)

▶ Print on the Aida cloth insert of hand towels, using permanent fabric ink. (Terry cloth isn't a good stamping surface.)

▶ Print in clay (see later in this chapter) to make pins or buttons.

▶ See the Easter card project in Chapter 3. The stamp used for the grass on the card is the Aquarium

Fig. 5-7

Grass stamp used on the shower curtain (Fig. 5-7, © Mostly Animals). (What's good for the fish is good for the eggs.)

♦ Substitute either DecoArt Ultra Gloss Acrylic Enamel (or DEKA Gloss Air) for glass stain. Ink with a cosmetic wedge. It's not necessary to apply a sealer before printing (see step 7), but a sealer over the print may be necessary. Clean all ink from the stamps immediately after printing. You may need to use a solvent-based stamp cleaner to remove all ink from the dies.

Shrink Plastic

There are several stamps used in other projects that can be used on this type of plastic. Shrink plastic reduces in size at about a 6 to 1 factor. That is, a print that is 6″ long and wide will be slightly larger than 1″ when the plastic is baked. This type of plastic comes with complete instructions on its correct usage. Follow the instructions exactly. When the print isn't big enough to shrink (for example, see Fig. 5-8, © Mostly Animals), but it's perfect for shrink plastic use (earrings, pins, bracelets, card embellishments, etc.), adhesive vinyl can be used as a substitute. One warning: Fake shrink plastic cannot be laundered.

Fig. 5-8

Remove covering from adhesive side. Print on adhesive side with a permanent ink. (Do not use inks labeled "washable" or "child-safe.") After the ink has completely dried, use permanent markers to color the print.

Allow the prints to dry. Cut another piece of adhesive vinyl the size of the print. Remove the covering from the adhesive side. Place the adhesive side of the second piece of vinyl over the print (adhesive side to adhesive side). Roll a pencil or skewer over both sides. Cut out the print along the outer edges. Use the fine side of an emery board to smooth any rough edges.

If you need a small hole for a jewelry finding, put the print on a piece of cardboard and push a needle through the print into the cardboard.

STAMPING ON CLAY

Clay likes to stick to dies. This problem is eliminated if the die is inked with glycerine or embossing ink before pressing it into the clay. Make a couple of prints on paper to remove the glycerine or embossing ink from the die.

Buy glycerine at the drugstore at the same time you buy the round foam (or latex) cosmetic sponges to use as a pad. Apply the glycerine to the top of the sponge. It'll take about five minutes to soak in. The pad won't dry out for months and months, if ever. Use the pad as you would use any inked pad.

A stamp has to be pushed firmly and evenly into clay for a good impression. Use the same board on the back of the block that's used when printing large stamps (see "Incomplete Prints" in Chapter 6). Place one hand on each end and push the stamp into the clay.

Rolling Clay

Potters use a simple method to roll a slab of clay evenly, and we might as well do it here the way the pros do. You'll need some kind of roller. Mine is very fancy—a 12″ length of thick-walled 1″ PVC pipe. See if the plumbing section of the hardware store has some odds and ends laying around.

You'll also need dowels. The ⅛″ and ¼″ widths are the most useful, but get an assortment of widths if you do a lot of clay projects. Cut the dowels in 12″ lengths.

Using a double layer of cooking parchment paper is a frustration saver. You don't have to peel the clay off the board before baking. Instead, the clay stays on the parchment paper for rolling, printing, baking, and cooling. No more finger-printed clay projects.

Clay usually needs to be worked and softened before rolling. Most need to be de-aired or de-bubbled (so that the clay doesn't look like it has a bad case of warts after baking). Follow the directions for the brand of clay you've selected.

Put a double layer (one piece on top of another) of cooking parchment on a flat surface and tape it down securely. Place one cut piece of doweling on either side of the paper. The dowels should about 8″ apart and parallel to each other. Put the clay between the doweling. To keep the clay from sticking to the roller, wipe the roller with a damp paper towel. Lay the roller on top of the doweling and roll over the clay. As the clay flattens, the width of the doweling will control the width of the rolled clay. As long as you keep the roller on the two pieces of doweling as you roll out the clay, the clay cannot be any thinner than the width of the doweling. If clay does not extend above the doweling, it won't be any thicker than the dimension of the doweling.

If you like a heavier roller than the PVC pipe, slide a dowel inside the PVC pipe, then push a cork into each end of the pipe. Don't use a skinny dowel—you want fat for weight.

Curing Clay

Oven-baked Clay

Follow the manufacturer's direction for the temperature of the oven and the type of baking sheet to use. Preheat the oven. When you're ready to bake the clay, pick up both pieces of doweling. Remove the tape from the cooking parchment paper. Pick up both ends of the paper and put it on the baking sheet. Do not remove the clay from cooking parchment paper until the clay is cool.

Air-dried Clay

When you're ready to dry the clay, pick up both pieces of doweling. Remove the tape from the cooking parchment paper. Pick up both ends of the paper and put it on a cake cooling rack. Don't remove the clay from the cooking parchment paper until the clay is thoroughly dry.

Terrific Tiles

When I saw this stamp, I couldn't wait to use it to make clay tiles. The results gave me another excuse to jump up and down. Don't limit tiles to the top of a wooden box. The rim of clay flower pots, buttons, jewelry, and tie tacks are all good uses for tiles (Fig. 5-9).

Needless to say, this stamp needn't be limited to clay. Use it for prints on a pillow cover or for embossed prints on a picture mat. Try it also on scarves and ties.

Fig 5-9

Supplies

P.O. Box Rubberstamps: Columbian Tile

One bar of brown Pro-Mat (or brand and color of your choice)

Round foam cosmetic sponge inked with glycerine (or embossing-ink pad)

Butter knife (without serrated edge)

Small wooden box with cover (square or rectangular in shape)

Sealer (clear or tinted)

Small disposable brush or cosmetic wedge

Mounting film

Supplies for rolling clay: two 12″ lengths of ¼″ doweling; 12″ piece of PVC pipe; cooking parchment paper

Baking sheet (type recommended on clay label)

Directions

1 Measure the top of the box. Determine how many tiles will be needed to cover the top. The tiles should be placed closely together.

2 Roll clay to a ¼″ thickness on a double layer of cooking parchment paper (see "Rolling Clay," above).

3 Ink the stamp on the glycerine pad.

4 Press the stamp into the clay, leaving a slight (⅛″) space between each print. It's not a bad idea to print a couple of extras, just in case.

5 Cut away the excess clay around the outer edges of the tiles with a knife. Be careful not to cut the cooking parchment paper. Do not remove the tiles from the paper.

6 Pick up the cooking parchment paper and place it on the baking sheet. Bake the clay according to the manufacturer's directions. Leave the tiles on the paper until they're thoroughly cool.

7 While the tiles are baking and cooling, sand the box and brush a sealer coat over all the sides and edges. Painting or decorating the inside of the box is optional. Allow to dry.

8 To make sure you have enough tiles, arrange them on the cover of the box. Remove the tiles.

9 Place the cover of the box, top down, on the mounting film. Trace the outer edges of the cover on the paper covering the top of the mounting film. Put an X in the center of the traced lines. (This will ensure that you remove the paper from the correct side of the film.) Cut along the traced lines.

10 Turn the cover over, right side up. Remove the paper with the X marking from the mounting film. Place it adhesive side down on top of the cover.

11 Remove the paper covering from the top of the mounting film. Position the tiles on the mounting film. Press the tiles into the adhesive.

Fine Feline Fellas

I think each of us needs a pin made from a clay print of this stamp (Fig. 5-10, © Quarter Moon Rubber Stamps). A print could also be used on a magnet, on a shirt pocket, or on top of a wooden box. But a pin would be my first choice.

Fig. 5-10

Supplies

Quarter Moon Rubber Stamps: Cool Cats

½ bar of white Glamour Cernit #1 (or brand and color of your choice)

Round foam cosmetic sponge inked with glycerine (or embossing-ink pad)

Butter knife (without serrated edge)

Pin back (purchase at crafts store)

Permanent glue suitable for use on polymer clay or mounting film

Cooking parchment paper and pipe or dowelling for rolling clay

Baking sheet (type recommended on clay label)

Metallic markers labeled suitable for plastic surfaces (optional)

Directions

1 Roll clay to a ¼″ thickness (see "Rolling Clay," p. 48).

2 Ink the stamp on the glycerine pad. Press the stamp into the clay.

3 Use the knife to cut away any excess clay from the outer edges of the print. Try not to cut the cooking parchment paper. Leave the clay on the paper.

4 Pick up the cooking parchment paper and place it on the baking sheet. Bake the clay according to the manufacturer's directions. Leave the clay on the paper until the clay is thoroughly cool.

5 Color the Cats' shirts with metallic markers. Allow to dry.

6 Attach the pin back to the print with permanent glue or mounting film.

☛ *Note:* Air-dried clay can also be used. Leave the clay on the parchment paper until dry; then color with the markers (don't use metallic markers). Apply protective finish to the clay after the markers are dry.

One of Fifty

I can't imagine a better teaching aide for geography and social studies than the state stamps from Mail Order Marking. What makes them unusual is their large size. Getting the complete set for your children's school could be a project for the parent's organization.

The stamps don't have to be limited to the classroom. Home state pride is something we all get into (some states a little more than others). I made a clay pin with the New Mexico stamp (Fig. 5-11). You could do the same with the stamp of your home state or make prints on shirts, caps, and jackets.

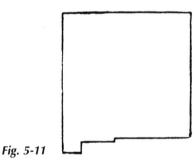

Fig. 5-11

Supplies

Mail Order Marking: Stamp of your state

Small amount of Fimo clay; a little more for Texas, Alaska, and California (Read the label on the clay for the required oven temperature when baking; 265 degrees is needed to melt Tinsel or Foil Embossing Powder.)

Round foam cosmetic sponge inked with glycerine (or embossing-ink pad)

Tinsel or Foil Embossing Powder (color of your choice)

Scrap paper

Supplies for rolling clay: two 12″ lengths of ¼″ doweling; 12″ length of PVC pipe; cooking parchment paper

This collection shows just a few of the many creative options available when stamping on paper. Photo frames and greeting cards using Frame Cards were designed by All Night Media, Inc.; cards, birth announcement, book mark, and gift tag were designed by Hampton Art Stamps, Inc.

This antiqued-finished slat-wood wall rack was printed with stamps available from All Night Media, Inc. The stamps were inked with acrylic craft paint.

Kalena K. Blakemore applies appliqués of stamped clay to the clay mugs she designs and sells. Her address is given in Supply Sources.

Two printed potholders designed by Hampton Art Stamps, Inc. Quilting "stitches" were made with a fine-tipped marker.

The gift wrap, tag, and pop-up card were designed by Hampton Art Stamps, Inc. The rubber stamps shown are from Great Notions Rubber Stamps.

Acrylic craft paint was used to ink the stamps for printing on these dried gourds. The polymer stamps in the foreground are from Pelle's See-Thru Stamps.

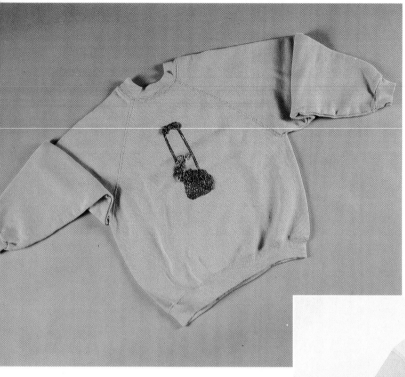

Puff paste was added to fabric paint for inking the large basket stamp printed on this sweatshirt. After the paint/puff mix had dried, heat was applied to the print. Silk flowers were handstitched in place. This stamp is available from First Impression Rubber Stamp Arts.

Museum of Modern Rubber has a kit with supplies and instructions for making Picture Puzzle Cubes. The cube shown was designed by Museum of Modern Rubber.

Vesta Abel used Jumbo Stamps from Comotion Rubber Stamps, Inc. to create this assortment of shrink art jewelry.

Pele Fleming, Pelle's See-Thru Stamps, designed this charming miniature quilt. Needless to say, it takes less time to stamp a miniature quilt than to stitch one.

Tree: *Clearsnap, Inc. stamps printed on Origami papers provided the "ornaments" and "lights" (several were thermal embossed). Beading wire was used as hooks for the ornaments; the lights were glued to 1/8" wide ribbon. Cross-locked beads and sequins were used as garlands. The star, from P.O. Box Rubberstamps, was glued to the top of the tree.*
Box: *After painting a basswood box with acrylic craft paint, a thermal embossed print was added to the lid. The large flower stamp from Raindrops on Roses was inked with embossing ink and printed. Tinsel embossing powder was sprinkled over the wet print and heat was applied to the powder.*

This party invitation and the colorful tap dancers designed by Donnie England, Quarter Moon Rubber Stamps, have an added plus. Magnetic sheeting was applied to the backs of the dancers; the dancers will hang around long after the party. Rubber stamp artist: Barbara Cressman.

YOU'RE INVITED!
DATE: JULY 17
TIME: 3 PM
PLACE: SUSIE'S
FOR: A PARTY!!!

Daisy prints decorate both the romper suit and the dress. Notice the daisy print stitched to the center front of the dress (right). To make this adorable little dress, cut away the bottom half of an infant-sized undershirt. With right sides together, stitch slightly gathered gingham fabric to the cut edge of the undershirt. Turn under the bottom edge of the gingham and hem. Dress and romper suit were designed by Pele Fleming, Pelle's See-Thru Stamps.

What child wouldn't love a pillow and pajamas stamped with dinosaurs? Both items were designed by Stamp Craft.

PERSONALIZE & DECORATE

Bookplate: *Make several prints of bookplates on sticker paper to give as gifts to the person who has everything. Remember to leave space for their name at the bottom of the print.*

Eyeglasses Case: *Another gift that takes little time is an eyeglasses case. Cut out four pieces of velvet in the size needed for the case. Stamp on two pieces. Stitch the pieces together then turn right side out. Slip stitch opening. (Artist rendition of stamp available from Ad-Lib.)*

Gina Gillen

Make a pillow for a friend and "quilt" with a fine-tipped marker. (Artist rendition of stamp available from Mail Order Marking.)

FACES
(OR ARMS OR LEGS!)

Tatoos wash off completely when stamps are inked with face paint. (Artist rendition of stamp available from All Night Media.)

PAPER & FABRIC

CLAY & PLASTIC

Framed Quilt: *Color the sashing of this quilt after pressure embossing. Then print and color the quilt blocks within the open areas. Instructions for this project are found in Chapter 3. (Artist rendition of plastic stencil available from American Traditional Stencils and stamps available from Pelle's See-Thru Stamps.)*

Bracelet: *Using clay for air drying, stamp and cut out each print. Allow clay to dry. Color clay prints with markers then apply a sealer over the colored prints. Glue the prints to a bracelet form with permanent glue. (Artist rendition of stamps available from Stamp Craft.)* **Pin:***Color a print made on Bristol Board then apply adhesive vinyl to both sides of the print. Cut out the print along the outer edges and glue a pinback to the back.*

Belt: *Cut pastel-colored cotton gauze fabric in the length and width desired for a tie-belt. Hem edges. Use an opaque fabric paint to ink the stamps. (Artist rendition of stamps available from Stuck on Stamps on belt and shoes.)*

Slacks: *To add printed strips to the side seams and across the pockets of slacks, cut fabric strips slightly wider than a roller stamp. Side seam strips should be the length from the bottom of the waist band to the lower edge of the cuff; strips for the pockets should be as long as the pocket top is wide. Apply a fusible web to the wrong side of each cut strip. Cut off fusible web extending beyond the edges of the strips. Turn strips over and print with the roller stamp. Fuse the strips to the side seams and pocket tops. Some fusibles will require your stitching or applying fabric paint along the outer edges of the strips. (Artist rendition of Rollagraph Stamp Wheel.)*

Jean Jacket: *The yoke of a denim jean jacket is perfect for a stamped lace design. Add some prints to the inside of the jacket back, too. Use an opaque white fabric paint to ink the stamp. Remember to pretest before printing on the jacket. (Artist rendition of stamp available from Stuck on Stamps.)*

Silk Scarf: *Brush a transparent fabric paint over a pre-hemmed silk scarf and allow to dry. Print with floral design stamps inked with a metallic fabric paint.*

Shoes: *Canvas shoes can be decorated quickly with stamps inked with either fabric paint or enamel markers.*

Plastic Sun Visor: *To decorate a visor brim with prints, ink stamps with either acrylic craft paints or a solvent-based stamp ink labeled "for plastic." Use the same stamps for printing the front of a shirt.*

Pocket T-shirt: *Make several prints on Dritz Iron-On Mending Fabric; color the prints with permanent markers. After cutting out the prints, arrange them on a shirt front. Fuse in place. (Artist rendition of stamp available from Pelle's See-Thru Stamps.)*

Sweatshirt: *Carousel animal stamps available from Mostly Animals (two are shown in this rendition) are always a colorful addition to a sweatshirt.*

Butter knife (without serrated edge)

Pin back (purchase at crafts store)

Permanent glue suitable for use on oven-baked clay or mounting film

Directions

1 Sprinkle a thin layer (as evenly as possible) of Tinsel or Foil Embossing Powder over the center of the cooking parchment paper. Place the piece of clay on top of the Tinsel or Foil.

2 Roll the clay to a ⅛″ thickness over the Tinsel or Foil. When the clay is flat and evenly rolled, turn it over. The clay should have a thin, even coating of the Tinsel or Foil Embossing Powder. Sprinkle Tinsel or Foil over any bare spots in the clay.

3 Ink the stamp on the glycerine pad. Make one print on scrap paper.

4 Press stamp into Tinsel (or Foil) side of the clay.

5 Cut any excess clay away from the outer edges of the print with a knife. Take care not to cut the cooking parchment paper. Leave the clay on the paper.

6 Pick up the cooking parchment paper and place it on a baking sheet. Bake according to the manufacturer's directions. Leave the clay on the paper until the clay is thoroughly cool.

7 If you want, glue a small acrylic jewel in the print to indicate your hometown.

8 Attach the pin back to the back of the pin with glue or mounting film.

STAMPING ON GOURDS, FROSTING, AND FUN FOAM

Gourds

Use a craft saw to cut off the neck from a dried gourd (or it can be left on). Print with permanent ink. Because the dried gourds look like old pots, I usually select stamps of either Petroglyph or Native American designs (Fig. 5-12, top two © Pelle's, bottom © Great Notions).

Frosting

I've been told that both stamps and stencils are great tools to use when decorating cakes and cookies. Since my one venture into the world of cake decorating was beyond the classification of a disaster, I'm hardly the one to give out advice.

But for those who can turn out a creation that doesn't look like a train that's been involved in a major collision in the oven; or a train that wasn't determined to turn south when the plate was westbound; or one that

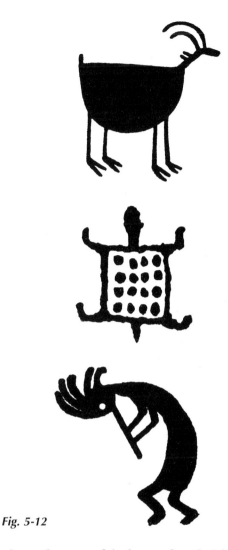

Fig. 5-12

doesn't require most of the boxes of toothpicks a grocery store has on the shelves to hold the layers of the cake together—stamps would be a handy tool, one light push into the frosting is all that's needed, so they tell me.

I could probably handle putting a stencil on top of a cake that was frosted in the pan, or putting a brass stencil on top of a cookie. Sprinkling colored sugar over a stencil can't be that difficult, can it (Fig. 5-13)?

I don't know. After the great train wreck, I left cake decorating to the experts.

MAKE A GOOD COOKIE EVEN BETTER!

Fig. 5-13

And now my children know why the cakes I made were always frosted in the pan. By the way, my son Dave's birthday party was a huge success—even with the cake. As the engine and the cars continued their southbound journey, most of the toothpicks popped up through the frosting. The three- and four-year-olds who were there were so impressed. They'd never seen a wooden cake.

Fun Foam

Look for the Westrim Crafts label on the back of the sheet of Fun Foam. Fun Foam is easier to print on and color than other brands. I haven't the faintest idea why.

Childrens' Projects

Clowning Around

Here's a project you and the children can do together. I'm not sure which is the most fun, the planning, the printing, or the finished project. This is an inexpensive toy that doesn't take long to make (Fig. 5-14).

Fig. 5-14

Supplies

Stuck On Stamps: Circus Clowns (The kit contains nine pieces that can be combined to create twenty-seven clowns.)

Foam pad or substitute with permanent ink

One sheet of white Fun Foam

One 12″ × 18″ piece of ½″-thick foam core—size of board can be enlarged or reduced (Foam core with adhesive side can be substituted; purchase at crafts store.)

One 12″ × 18″ piece white felt (same size as board)

⅓ yard of ½″-wide heavy-duty hook-and-loop tape

Permanent fabric glue (mounting film optional)

Permanent markers, assorted colors

1⅔ yard of ½″-wide trim (long enough to go around edges of board)

Scissors

Large-eye needle and ribbon or pearl cotton (optional)

Directions

1   Using fabric glue, attach the felt to one side of the foam core.

2   For a handle (optional): Fold the trim in half, end to end. Mark the halfway point. Thread a needle with ribbon or pearl cotton. Put a large knot in one end. Put the needle through the wrong side of the trim at the halfway marking and pull the knot tightly against the wrong side of the trim. Put the needle back through the right side of the trim. The distance should be wide enough for the handle to slip easily over the child's hand. Make a large knot on the thread. Pull the knot up against the wrong side of the trim.

3   Attach trim around edges of board with either glue or mounting film. (I prefer the mounting film.) The handle should be in the center of one edge.

4   Print the clown pieces on the Fun Foam. Color the prints.

5   Cut out the prints, cutting ⅛″ from those areas that would be difficult to cut out exactly.

6   Attach the hook side of the tape (the more bristly of the two) to the entire back of each cut-out print. (I use mounting film.)

7   That's it. When the tape gets filled up with fuzzies from the felt, clean it off with a toothbrush.

Now, what's to be done with the loop half of the tape? Mount the pieces on a block and use this "stamp" for background prints (see "Background Prints" in Chapter 6).

Pet Rocks

Any of the Trolls included in the Hampton Art Stamps catalog would do a good job of turning a plain, everyday rock into a pet (Fig. 5-15, © 1993 Hampton Art Stamps). The only thing this pet has to have is a reasonably smooth surface. Add personality with paints and markers. Apply a protective finish over nonpermanent inks, paints, and markers.

Fig. 5-15

Faces, Legs, and Arms

Palmer Face Paint is the ink to use for body printing (commonly known as tattoos). Fortunately, these tattoos are temporary; soap and water quickly removes the prints. But the question "What am I going to be for Halloween?" is easier to answer with a couple of stamps, a foam pad or substitute, and this paint.

© Comotion Rubber Stamps, Inc.

6

TIPS AND TRICKS

The methods that follow are just the tip of the iceberg. Don't stop here. You'll discover other methods each time you pick up a stamp.

The topics are arranged in alphabetical order so that you can find them quickly. The techniques described in this chapter can be substituted in many of the projects included in Chapters 3, 4, and 5.

BACKGROUND PRINTS

Rather than confuse the issue, foreground, background, and texture prints will be referred to as background prints. (Fig 6-1 shows two prints made with texture stamps, Stuck on Stamps © 1993.) The purpose of background prints is to add perspective and/or to fill in blank spaces surrounding a stamped design.

A background does not have to be printed with a stamp (see "Colored Pencils, Pastel Chalk, Water Color Pencils, and Wax Crayons," (p. 55); "Sponge Stamps" in Appendix A). Even when dry, watercolors (markers and brushed colors) can be blended together with a damp sponge (or a computer cleaning swab, the end of a wedge-shaped cosmetic sponge, etc.). Watercolors flow into an area that has been brushed with a damp sponge. A second color can be added on top of the first.

Sponges are often used for "printing" open areas. Any type of sponge or foam works. The type of sponge, the type of ink, and the manner of inking is determined by the effect you want to achieve.

A round cosmetic sponge can be wiped across an inked pad; the side of a marker can be stroked over the end of a wedge-shaped cosmetic sponge; the end of a

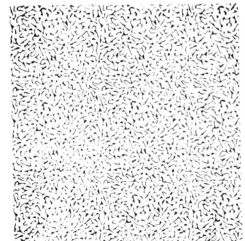

Fig. 6-1

computer cleaning sponge can be dipped into diluted fabric paint or liquid watercolor; the surface of a sponge can be inked with a rubber roller (brayer). See Appendix C for additional ways of inking sponge and foam supplies.

To create a shaded color, wipe the tip of a dark-colored marker (permanent or watercolor) on the sides and tip of a light-colored marker. Roll the tip of the lighter marker on paper to remove the darker color.

Other supplies can also be used to create dimension in a design either before or after printing, for example a Splatter Brush, Designer Dots, or Decorating Set (all from Kemper), or a Wood Graining Tool or Combing Tool from Accent. The desired effect determines the best ink and tool to use. After printing a winter scene, for instance, brush or splatter white crystal fabric paint on the print. Sponge or brush a thin fabric paint (for example, DEKA-Silk, FabricArts, Tumble-Dye) over the surface before printing a design. Spray either nontextured fabric paint or craft paint before printing the design; spray textured (glitter, for example) after printing the design. Almost any type of ink (including embossing ink) can be applied with the Splatter Brush.

The type of ink used, as well as the design, determine when to apply the background. For example, embossing ink and embossing powders generally are applied after a design has been printed and colored.

COLORED PENCILS, PASTEL CHALK, WATER-COLOR PENCILS, AND WAX CRAYONS

There are times when a colored pencil is easier to use than a marker. The sharp point of a pencil easily colors anything that's tiny (flowers, leaves, pieces in a quilt block, etc.). Children usually have better results with colored pencils.

Pastel chalk and watercolor pencils have a softer lead than regular colored pencils and are excellent to use for coloring prints and backgrounds. The softer lead can be blended to create darker and lighter shades. Either General's Pastel Chalk Pencils or General's Kimberly Water Soluble Color Pencils (water color pencils) can be blended with a makeup applicator. General's Kimberly Water Soluble Color Pencils can also be blended with a damp makeup applicator, sponge, or brush. Both pencils are erasable. You can purchase them in crafts and art supply stores.

When using softer lead pencils, cover completed portions with tracing paper as you work. The paper will protect the colored prints from smearing.

Colored pencils of any type can be stroked lightly on the paper. Light strokes won't cover the details of a print. Use the side, rather than the point, of the lead when coloring large areas. Use the point for fine details. All strokes should go in the same direction.

Sharpen colored pencils with a regular pencil sharpener, an old emery board, or an eyebrow pencil sharpener. (Wait for a Dollar Day Sale at the drugstore—you might be able to get two for $1.)

Spray a protective coating or fixative over projects colored with erasable pencils, watercolor or pastel chalk pencils. If the project is framed under glass or covered with adhesive vinyl, the protective coating is not necessary.

Sharpened wax crayons (use an eyebrow pencil sharpener for these, too) are an inexpensive way to color prints. Crayons can be used on fabric that will be laundered (cool water, line dry). Bond freezer paper to the wrong side of the fabric before printing (shiny side of paper on wrong side of fabric; silk setting on iron). The freezer paper holds the fabric stable so that it won't ruffle when coloring with the crayons.

Crayons used on fabric must be heat set. Cover the ironing board with tissue paper or a paper bag. Set the iron at the cotton setting. Turn the fabric over, freezer paper side up, and press at least fifteen seconds or until the wax is melted into the fabric (Fig. 6-2). Remove the freezer paper after heat setting.

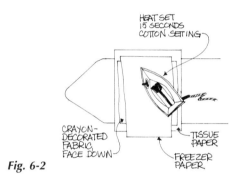

Fig. 6-2

China markers can be used just like wax crayons. (Most office-supply and crafts stores have them.) Those wax markers are wrapped in paper that you unwind to expose the point. They're great for children to use because they don't break as long as they stay wrapped (the wrapping protects the marker just as it does on a wax crayon). Children enjoy unwinding the paper covering, so be prepared.

About the best way to salvage unwrapped china markers is to melt them in a double boiler and make crayon chunks. Use spray shortening to coat the inside of hard candy molds; pour the melted china markers into the mold; remove when cool. Remember to use caution when melting—the wax catches fire at a low temperature.

At the risk of being yelled at by a lot of people, I'm going to tell you that markers, colored pencils, pastel pencils, wax crayons, and oil pastels sticks can all be used in one project. There are some limitations, however. Pencils and sticks should not be colored over with markers on some materials because of smearing or smudging. The combination can be used only on paper and wood. Apply either a protective finish or adhesive vinyl over the finished project.

My advice is to color prints and backgrounds with the supplies that are the easiest and fastest to use and that produce the results you want.

DIMENSIONAL EFFECTS

Perceived dimension, or depth, in a print or group of prints can be created with background prints or masking (see "Masking," later in this chapter). Actual dimension is created when something is attached behind a print or group of prints that have been cut out.

To create actual dimension simply print on paper, cut out the print, and apply a strip of 1/8"-wide double-faced sewing/craft tape to the center back of the print. Remove the paper covering the tape and stick the print down on the surface.

Butterfly wings can be bent forward; the petals and leaves of flowers can be curled. A reverse print (see "Reverse Prints," later in this chapter) can be used on the back for added effect.

Another way to create actual dimension is to attach a spacer to the back of a cut-out print. Place the print, spacer side down, on the surface. The spacer holds the print away from the surface (Fig. 6-3).

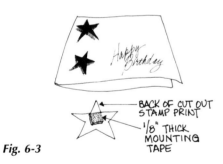

BACK OF CUT OUT
STAMP PRINT
1/8" THICK
MOUNTING
TAPE

Fig. 6-3

Print the design used for the cut-out print on the background before attaching the spacer. This is especially effective if the cut-out print is raised more than 1/8" above the background.

The length and width of a spacer has to be large enough to support the cut-out print. If poster board is used for a large flower print, a 1/4"-square piece of spacer material is not enough support (unless you like floppy flowers). The thickness of the spacer is determined by the distance you want between the background surface and the cut-out print. Usually the thickness should not be more than 1/2" on nonwearables and 1/4" on wearables.

An adhesive is needed on each side of the spacer. Mounting tape has an adhesive on each side, can be purchased either by the roll or in cut pieces, and is best

for those projects that won't be laundered. If desired, more than one thickness can be used.

Bristol board, foam core, cardboard, Fun Foam, the sponges used on the back of earrings, and styrofoam are excellent supplies to use as spacers for projects that won't be laundered. Use double-faced tape, mounting film, or glue to attach these items behind the cut-out print. (Some earring sponges have an adhesive on each side.)

Projects that will be laundered require spacers that can be laundered. For spacers, try batting, fused layers of fabric, flat buttons, and thinly rolled pieces of baked clay (Fimo or Sculpey, for example). Permanent fabric glue or fusible web must be used as the adhesive.

EASY CUTTING

You do a lot of cutting when you're working with stamps. The right tool for the job is the first requirement for easy cutting. Cutting tools most used are scissors (small- and medium-sized blades), rotary cutters, and craft knives (Fig. 6-4).

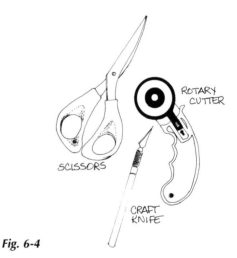

ROTARY
CUTTER

SCISSORS

CRAFT
KNIFE

Fig. 6-4

Here are some ways to make cutting out prints easier.

- First cut to 1/4" of the outside edges of a print. Then cut on the outer edges.

- Keep the blades of the scissors perpendicular to your body. Rotate what you're cutting; don't rotate the scissors. Resting your arm on a flat surface will help break the "swinging scissors" habit.

- Keep the line you are cutting to the left of the blades as much as possible (to the right, if you're left-handed).

- If the outer edges of the design are a maze of itty-bitty ins and outs, don't even try to cut them. Instead, cut about 1/8" from the outer edges (Fig. 6-5).

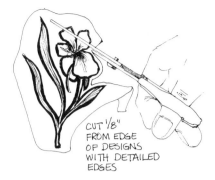

Fig. 6-5

CUT ⅛"
FROM EDGE
OF DESIGNS
WITH DETAILED
EDGES

Scissors

Don't worry about cutting paper with your good scissors. Paper won't dull scissors any faster than fabric. Always wipe blades after use, regardless of what was cut.

Small craft scissors clip around nooks and crannies. The sharper the points, the better.

If you prefer using one pair of scissors for everything, take a look at a Fiskars Softouch Micro-tip, a mid-size scissors suitable for paper, fabric, softer plastics, thin balsa wood, and foam.

Rotary Cutters

Rotary cutters are timesavers for almost every craft or sewing activity (see Appendix F, Rotary Paper Trimmer). Straight, wavy, pinking, and perforated blades are available for all rotary cutter handles. The size of the blade determines the thickness it will cut. The larger-size blades cut through several layers of paper, fabric, soft plastic, thin balsa wood, and thin foam (provided, of course, the blade is reasonably new and sharp).

Substitute for Rotary Cutter

If you don't have a rotary cutter, you can use a tracing wheel and Fun Foam (here's one time you can use a substitute brand) to cut light weight papers. A serrated edge seam marker produces one type of cut; a Clover blunt edge tracing wheel produces another; a double-seam marker cuts narrow strips.

Place a sheet of Fun Foam under the paper you are cutting. Cut next to a straight edge (ruler) or curved edge (French curve) to make it easier. I'll warn you, the Fun Foam gets cut up, too. But that's the best surface I've found to use as a cutting mat for tracing wheels.

Craft Knives

Craft knives do the jobs not intended for scissors and rotary cutters. Handles and blades are available in every size and shape imaginable (including saw blades). Purchase them in crafts and hobby stores (see Hobby Supplies and Arts and Crafts Supplies in Appendix F).

Cutting Accurate Corners with a Craft Knife

Use a small craft knife to cut accurate corners (both inner and outer) for all surfaces except fabric and hard wood.

▶ Hold the knife perpendicular to the surface. Push the point of the craft knife into the surface at the corner marking.

▶ Bring the handle of the knife down toward the surface, pushing the blade into the surface along the marked line (Fig. 6-6). The cut should not be any longer than the blade. Take out the knife.

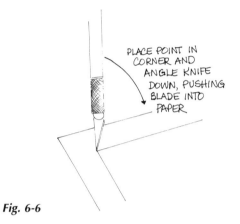

PLACE POINT IN
CORNER AND
ANGLE KNIFE
DOWN, PUSHING
BLADE INTO
PAPER

Fig. 6-6

▶ Rotate the paper so that you can easily see the markings on the other side of the corner. Push the point of the knife into the corner again, at the same spot as before. Push the blade into the surface along the marked line of that side. Take out the knife.

▶ Repeat these steps for each corner of the shape.

▶ Cut the remainder of each marked line with either scissors or a craft knife.

▶ Slide the blade of the knife (or use a pin) under the cut-out piece. It should lift right out. The corners will be cut exactly as they were marked.

Another Cutting Tool

The Fiskars Diagonal Craft Cutter isn't a craft knife, but it's far more than a scissors. It cuts everything from paper to rubber dies to fine wire.

ECHO PRINTS

I haven't the faintest idea what these are supposed to be called, so I call them Echo Prints. I suppose Shadow Prints would be O.K., too. Whatever you call them, they're an effective and quick way to add interest to a printed design.

Ink the stamp and make one print. Don't re-ink. Make one overlapping print after another until there's no ink left on the die (Fig. 6-7, © Mostly Animals).

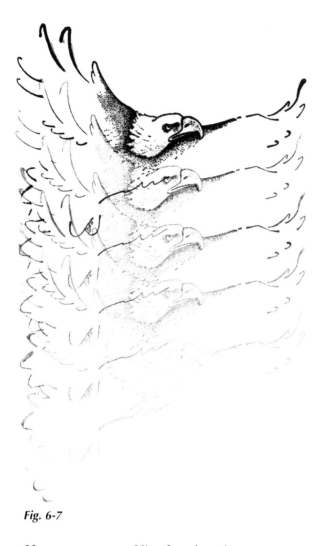

Fig. 6-7

If you want a curved line for echo prints, trace a very light pencil line next to a curved guide (French curve, plate, cup, etc.). If you want a straight line, use a straight edge for the tracing guide. You can also use a positioning tool (see "Positioning Tools," later in this chapter).

Position the bottom of the block along the drawn line or against the side of a positioning tool when printing. If you want the prints evenly spaced, use a part of the design as a register mark for positioning the block (see the Halloween card in Chapter 3).

PRESSURE EMBOSSING ON PAPER

Pressure embossing creates a raised design on the right side of the paper. Coloring the embossed design is optional. Plain, inexpensive stationery, note cards, and envelopes acquire a special look when embossed. It takes about one minute to emboss a monogram.

In addition to paper, an embossing tool (stylus), a stencil (either colored plastic or brass), and either removable tape or repositionable glue are required for embossing paper.

If you plan to color the embossed design, use either markers, colored pencils, oil pastel sticks, or stencil paint (see "Colored Pencils, Pastel Chalk, Watercolor Pencils, and Wax Crayons," p. 55, and "Oil Pastel Sticks and Semi-solid Stencil Paints," later in this chapter).

Embossing Tools

Just about any weight paper can be embossed. The secret is in the tool (Fig. 6-8). The tip of an embossing tool can be anything from a hard, ball-shape to one that is soft and rounded. Tissue paper can be embossed with the tip of a dried-up marker. Computer or typing paper can be embossed with a Dritz Ball Point Bodkin (normally used to pull cording or elastic through a casing). Heavier papers such as construction paper and handmade papers can be embossed with traditional embossing tools. One-hundred-pound bristol board (usually in tablets) can be embossed with a dry ballpoint pen. The embossing tool should not penetrate or tear the paper. If it does, the tip is too small or has a sharp edge.

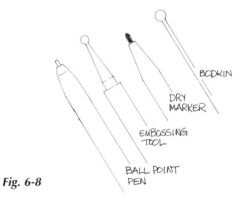

BODKIN

DRY MARKER

EMBOSSING TOOL

BALL POINT PEN

Fig. 6-8

Light Tables

A light table isn't required, but it makes things easier. The substitute is a window. (You need light behind the stencil.) But a window requires that you stand when embossing, and you're limited to embossing during the daytime. If you enjoy embossing, consider getting a light table.

In the past, light tables were not used much for sewing and craft activities because they were expensive, heavy, and fragile. Now, Me Sew, Inc., and American Traditional have light tables that are reasonably priced, lightweight, and sturdy. American Traditional also has available videos describing methods for making your own light tables.

Me Sew, Inc., Light Tables (Fig. 6-9) have clips that hold stencil/paper layers in place on the table. On the American Traditional Light Table, use long bobby pins (the really long ones without ridges) to hold the layers in place. Place a piece of scrap paper under the bobby pins, because they can leave pressure marks on some papers.

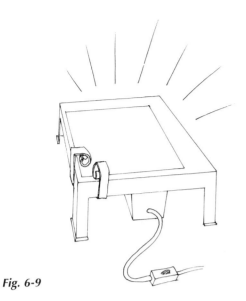

Fig. 6-9

Windows

If you prefer using a window, attach the stencil on the paper securely. Then use either removable or low-tack tape to attach the stencil/paper layers to the window.

Removable Tape and Repositionable Glue

Stencils can be secured to a surface (paper, fabric, walls, etc.) with removable or low-tack tape. Frankly, I think tape is one big pain—repositionable glue is so much easier to use. Spray glue and marker glue are a little faster to apply than a brushed-on liquid repositionable glue.

Follow the directions on the can of spray stencil glue to apply it to the back of the stencil. If using marker glue, wipe the marker over the back of the stencil. Let the glue dry until it looks dull (about ten minutes). You'll be able to use the stencil at least eight times before it needs another coat of glue.

Use a solvent-based stamp cleaner to remove repositionable glue (spray, marker glue, or liquid) from the back of the stencil. Place the stencil on three or four layers of paper towels, back up. Wipe the cleaner over the glue (and all the other junk that's on the stencil). Let it set about ten minutes. Rinse the stencil under warm water. If any glue remains on a plastic stencil, gently scrub it off with a Teflon-safe scouring pad. Any glue remaining on a brass stencil can be wiped off with a dry paper towel.

As long as we're on the subject of stencils, this is the place to mention displaying brass stencils. These beautiful brass creations are far too pretty to stick in a box in a drawer. Colored mat board can be cut to the size needed for each stencil. Put a small hanger on the back of the cut mat board. If you used repositionable glue on the back of the stencil, stick it right on the mat board. If you didn't use glue on the back, a sequin pin (they're really tiny) can be put into the front of the mat board and used as a hanger for the stencil. Brass stencils are also a nice addition to stamps displayed on shelves (especially if you shine them up periodically with brass polish).

TIPS FOR EMBOSSING ON PAPER

It isn't necessary that you emboss the entire stencil design. Tape dark paper over the areas you do not want to emboss. You'll be able to see those dark areas through the paper when embossing.

Apply repositionable glue to the back of the stencil. Place the stencil, right side down, on the light table or window. Place the paper, right side down, over the stencil. Smooth flat with your fingertips. On a light table, hold the layers in place with clips or bobby pins; on a window, attach the layers with tape.

If the stencil is attached with tape rather than glue, tape the stencil, right side down, to the light table or window. Place the paper, right side down, over the stencil. On a light table, hold the layers in place with clips or pins; on a window, attach the layers with tape.

Embossing Designs that are not Colored

Attach the paper to the stencil with either tape or glue. Attach the stencil/paper layers to either a light table or window. Push the tip of the tool against the edges of the stencil design with moderate pressure (Fig. 6-10). It's like tracing, except that you're not making a colored mark.

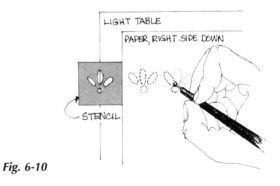

Fig. 6-10

Before lifting the paper from the stencil, check that all areas of the stencil are embossed. Run your fingers over the paper—you'll be able to feel the impressions made by the tool.

Embossing Designs that are Colored

Color the design before embossing. Secure the stencil, right side up, to the right side of the paper with either repositionable glue or removable tape. Color and allow to dry.

Without removing the stencil from the paper, turn the layers over. The right side of the stencil will be down. Place on either a light table or window. Secure as directed above. Emboss as directed for an uncolored design, above.

FANCY EDGES

Decorated edges can be made with markers, punches, embossing powders, foil, mylar, ribbon, and embellishments. Glue and fusible web can be used to attach items. Curved lines can be cut along an edge with scissors, a craft knife or a Rotary Paper Trimmer.

When you want just a hint of color along an edge, use a marker. Hold the marker with the tip up. Rest the edge of the paper on the plastic sleeve surrounding the bottom of the marker tip. The sleeve will support the paper so that you won't end up with marker squiggles all over the place. Run the marker around the edge of the paper (Fig. 6-11).

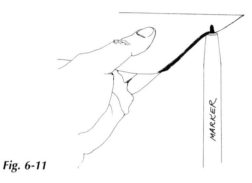

Fig. 6-11

Punched designs are another super-speedy fancy edge. McGill Punches have a deep reach, some as much as 2″. Marvy Uchida Craft Punches coordinate with many stamp prints.

Thermal embossing ranks as a speedy fancy edge. Use either an embossing marker or the brand of embossing ink that is in a fine-tip bottle (it looks like a writer tip bottle used for fabric paint). Apply a band of embossing ink, as wide as you want, along the edge of the paper. Sprinkle a layer of embossing powder on a piece of paper and dip the inked edge of the paper into it. Apply heat to the powder.

Foil can be applied to the edge of the paper with either glue or a fusible web (see "Fuse It" in Chapter 7). Brush foil glue along the edge with a small brush. Use as wide a band of glue as you want. Follow the manufacturer's directions for applying the foil. The glue and foil can be either the type limited to paper foiling or the type used for fabric foiling.

To use a fusible with foil, fuse narrow strips of a lightweight fusible to the edges of the paper. The iron should be at the synthetic setting. Remove the paper backing from the fusible. Place the foil, color side up,

over the fusible strip. Cover the foil with white tissue paper. Press. After the foil has cooled, secure a small piece of tape on one corner of the foil. Pick up the end of the tape. The tape will pull the clear covering off the top of the foil.

Mylar is available in sheets (wrapping paper), plain and punched ribbon, and pre-cut shapes. Any can be applied to the edge of paper with marker glue or fusible web. Gluing is simply a process of applying glue to the back of strips cut from the sheets, or on the ribbon or pre-cut shapes. Finger press down.

When using fusible web, place the mylar on an ironing board and cover with the fusible, paper side up. Place white tissue paper over the fusible. (Any mylar extending beyond the fusible has to be covered, too.) The iron should be at the synthetic setting.

Strips of mylar can be cut from sheets of wrapping paper after the fusible has been added. A rotary cutter or trimmer can quickly cut these strips. I like using a blade with either a wavy or pinking edge.

Place the fused side of the mylar on the paper you are decorating. Cover with white wrapping tissue. Press, using a synthetic setting. Remove the tissue when the fusible is cool.

If you don't want to mess with glue or fusibles, narrow mylar tape with an adhesive backing (sticky fashion tapes) can be purchased in crafts and art supply stores. It's handy having a couple of rolls in the house. A single strip puts zing into any design.

Embellishments (ribbon, glitter, sequins, buttons, laces, doilies, etc.) can be glued to paper. When you don't want to wait for the glue to dry, and the item isn't affected by heat, use a fusible web. Apply in the same way as used for mylar (low heat and tissue paper). Be sure to cover lace and doilies (or anything with holes) with tissue paper when fusing. The fusible in the holes will fuse to the tissue paper (Fig. 6-12). The tissue paper must be picked up immediately, while the fusible is still warm.

Mark designs for cut edges with a soft lead using stencils, curved rulers, the bottom of a glass, doilies, or anything you can run a pencil around. The marked lines should be very light. Use that same design on the envelope flap for a special touch. Then add an embossed monogram.

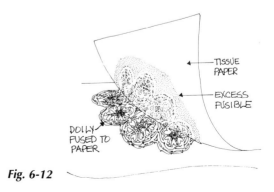

TISSUE PAPER

EXCESS FUSIBLE

DOILY FUSED TO PAPER

Fig. 6-12

Make a template for designs you use a lot. I use adhesive vinyl. In this case, I don't remove the covering from the adhesive side.

Chapter 7 has more information about adding glitz to paper, fabric, and wood.

FLAT KNOTS

Flat knots are useful when an envelope (or any packaging container) would flatten a puffy bow. When you get your copy of the Raindrops On Roses catalog (Appendix G), you'll see these handy tips:

- Punch two holes, an inch apart, at the top edge of the paper. (The holes can be closer or wider apart if you wish.)

- Thread both ends of the ribbon through the two holes from the front of the paper to the back.

- Bring both ends through the holes to the front of the paper. The ribbon crosses over in the back (Fig. 6-13).

GENTLY
PULL TIGHT
AND TRIM
ENDS

Fig. 6-13

This technique can also be used on the edges of printed paper or fabric that is fused to fabric, paper, or wood. Print the design. Apply fusible web to the wrong side of the printed paper or fabric. Do not remove the paper on the fusible—first punch the holes needed for the ribbon, then remove the paper. Place the ribbon in the holes (from front to the back, then through the front). Fuse the printed paper or fabric to the surface you're decorating. The fusible will hold the ribbon in place on the wrong side of the print. Apply a drop of glue to the cut ends of the ribbon to prevent fraying on fabric that will be laundered.

McGill Punches (Punch Line and Utility) punch through multiple layers of fabric, fusible web, and paper.

FOILED PRINTS

Paper and wood are excellent surfaces for foiled prints. Not all fabrics are good surfaces. The best fabrics are wovens (silk, rayon, cotton, and poly/cotton) and light-weight knits. Heavy or dense fabrics (sweatshirt fleece, denim, etc.) are not good surfaces for foiled prints.

Not every stamp design can be used with the glue used for the foil. Fine line designs don't pick up enough glue. Some stencil type or positive designs may not leave an even print of glue. Polymer stamps, regardless of the design, always seem to work well.

Ink with either a rubber roller that has been inked with an even layer of glue or on an inked freezer paper pad (see Appendix C). I've used marker glue to ink stamps, but the results vary with different brands of foil. Foils and glues that require heat setting don't work too well with stamp prints.

Check the die after inking. If there's an excess of glue, pat the die with a clean sponge. Foiling requires a few test prints before beginning a project, especially if you're printing on fabric.

Clean the glue from the die immediately after printing. A solvent-based cleaner and a toothbrush will remove bits of glue stuck in the die. Don't try to store pads inked with glue because it doesn't work. Rinse glue from the pad immediately after use.

Prints can be outlined with foil glue. Use a fine-line applicator tip (Plaid has a packaged assortment of these tips) or the syringe available from Rupert, Gibbon & Spider (see Appendix E) if the glue bottle does not have a small tip. Follow the directions on the glue bottle before applying the foil.

Remember that foil applied to fabric that will be laundered must be coated with a sealer for protection. Foiled items should not be machine washed and dried.

INCOMPLETE PRINTS

We all make them—consider them a part of stamping. Fill in the blank spots of a design with a marker. Two brands with a micro-tip are Y & C Permawriter II and Sakura Pigment Micron. Both are permanent and can be used on porous surfaces. Sakura Identi-Pens have a fine tip. These markers are permanent on several surfaces, including plastic. Read "Printing with Large Stamps," later in this chapter.

LABELS

Hand work of any type deserves a label, and you deserve recognition for your work. At the very least, include your name and the date it was completed. If the work is a gift, include the recipient's name, too.

In addition to stamps that are specifically designed for printing labels (Fig. 6-14, © 1993 Hampton [top] and © 1993 Delafield [bottom] and Fig. 6-15, © 1993 Pelle's), many stamp designs can be adapted for this purpose (Fig. 6-16, © 1993 Hampton).

Fig. 6-14

Fig. 6-15

Fig. 6-16

MARKERS

Markers are the stamper's paintbrush. Make sure that the right type of marker is used for the technique, the surface, and intended use of the project. Don't use a watercolor marker on a T-shirt; don't use a permanent marker to create a shaded watercolor effect on paper.

Use a soft touch when coloring with a marker. Stroke in one direction when possible. On broader tip markers, use the side of the tip rather than the point of the tip. Overcoloring will produce darker shades, and sometimes that isn't what you want.

On paper, use light strokes. Too much pressure will produce a ragged surface. Apply a spray fixative to the paper before coloring with markers to prevent "marker

run" (either the color takes off across the paper on a dead run, or one small apple ends up being one large weird-looking red thing).

Before using markers on fabric, bond freezer paper to the wrong side of the fabric. The freezer paper will hold the fabric stable. Leave the paper on the fabric until after heat setting—always heat set markers used on fabric. To prevent marker run on fabric, apply an antifusant before coloring with the markers.

Raw wood should be sealed before coloring with markers. Marker run can happen on wood, too, especially balsa wood. The sealer should not be too thick; the marker should penetrate the wood. After the marker is dry, spray on a protective finish.

MASKING

Masking is when a mask, or covering, is placed over a print or portion of a print for protection. You just don't get to put feathers and eyeholes on this kind of mask.

There are four ways to mask: with paper; with adhesive vinyl; with erasable markers; or masking the die itself.

Paper Mask

A paper mask is the traditional method of masking. Make a print of the selected stamp on the surface of the project and allow it to dry. Make a second print of that stamp on a piece of scrap paper and cut it out as accurately as possible around the outer edges. This cut-out print is the mask.

Place the mask over the print made on the project. Make a print with the next stamp. Remove the mask from the first print. Now the prints appear to overlap.

Fig. 6-19 (© Good Stamps.Stamp Goods) is the front of a card that was printed using a slightly different type of paper mask. A piece of paper, the same size as the front of a card, was irregularly torn. Both of the torn pieces were used as masks. The lower half of the torn paper was placed over the lower half of the card. The giraffes were printed on the upper half of the card. When the torn paper mask was removed, the giraffes were only printed on the top half of the card (Fig. 6-20).

The upper half of the torn paper was then placed over the upper half of the card. The grass stamp was printed across the bottom half of the card. When the torn paper mask was removed, the grass was only printed on the lower half of the card (see Fig. 6-19).

Fig. 6-17

Fig. 6-18

A mask allows you to print one design over another, as illustrated in Fig 6-17 (© Pelle's). If the second bear was printed over the first, or the bear was printed over the chair, the result would be a mess (Fig. 6-18, © Pelle's). To avoid this, a mask is placed over the first print before making the second print.

Fig. 6-19

Fig. 6-20

Adhesive Vinyl Mask

Masking instructions often tell you to make the mask from paper, but the only time I use a paper mask is for the technique described for the giraffe card, above. Paper doesn't hold up; it gets raggedy. As long as I'm going to the trouble of cutting out a print to use as a mask, I want it to last. So I use adhesive vinyl.

Adhesive vinyl cuts with scissors, is clear, and there's no worrying about it shifting when printing over it. Remember, though, that the adhesive is sticky. Stick it on and off fabric a few times to reduce the sticking power. (Then pretest its stickiness on scrap paper.)

If pigment ink is used, the print will wipe off the mask as you're using it. Because the vinyl is clear, you won't have any problem in positioning the mask. If you prefer a permanent print on the mask, use a solvent-based ink intended for hard surfaces to ink the die (see Appendix B). Clean the die immediately after use.

When I'm finished using an adhesive vinyl mask, I stick it over the index on wooden blocks or on the inside of plastic box blocks. The mask is handy whenever I want to use it. When necessary, I store them in my stamp directory (see Appendix A).

Erasable Marker Masking

When you don't want to spend time making a mask, this is the way to go. You'll need an erasable marker (Marvy Uchida Erasable Fluorescent with Eraser Tip and Y & C Eye-Popper Base Color and Eye-Popper Eraser are two brands) and a permanent marker. Removable fabric markers used for stitching cannot be used; they dry too quickly on the die.

Ink the first stamp with the erasable marker. Print on the project. Ink the stamp used for the second print with the permanent marker. Make the print with that stamp exactly where you want it on the design. The re-sults will look like the jumble shown in Fig. 6-18.

When the print made with the permanent marker is dry, use the eraser marker to erase conflicting lines of the first print (the one made with the erasable marker). The eraser and erasable marker must be the same brand. Allow the erasable marker to dry. Markers or colored pencils can then be used to color prints.

The erasable marker used for the first print is not permanent. When using the above method on a fabric that will be laundered, you'll have to overline the first print with a permanent marker after the erasable marker has dried. Use permanent markers to color the prints. Pretest—the erasable marker should easily erase from the fabric you have selected.

Masking the Die

Mask the die itself only if a stamp doesn't ink well with a marker. (Normally you use a marker when you only want to ink a portion of a die.) The design shouldn't be intricate—there has to be space between the portion of the die you are printing and the portion you are mask-ing. This method was used for printing the heart stamp used in the embossed Framed Quilt project in Chapter 3 (see Fig. 3-23).

Use a slow-drying ink (pigment ink, for example). Ink the stamp and then place strips of masking tape (what else?) over the areas you do not want to print. The strips of tape should be long enough to reach around to the back of the block. Print. What is covered with tape will not print.

To repeat the print, lift the tape before re-inking and replace the tape before printing. It's tedious, but it's one way to get around a problem.

OIL PASTEL STICKS AND SEMISOLID STENCIL PAINT

I've combined these two types of coloring agents in the same category because of their similarities. The consis-tency of each allows you to easily paint stencil designs.

- There's little chance of their seeping under the stencil.

- Colors can be blended on either the brush or the surface.

- Embossing powder can be applied, although it must be applied immediately to oil pastel sticks.

One difference is in their permanency. Sakura Cray-Pas Oil Pastel Sticks are not permanent. A pro-tective coating is needed if the project will be handled a lot (mail art, wooden boxes, walls, etc.). Delta Stencil Magic Paint Creme, Deco Art Easy Blend Stencil Paint, and Plaid Stencil Decor Dry Brush Stencil Paint are permanent on porous surfaces, including fabric.

After a lot of fiddling around, I found that a small scrubber brush used for fabric paint (DecoArt Brush Pen is available in two small sizes) produced the best results when painting small stencil designs.

Secure the stencil to the paper, wood, wall, or fabric (see "Tips for Embossing on Paper," p. 59). Rub the end of the brush across the oil pastel stick or stencil paint. (When working with an oil pastel stick, don't do this over the project—little flecks scatter all over.) When painting, hold the brush perpendicular to the top of the stencil. Twist and push the bristles into the stencil cuts (Fig. 6-21).

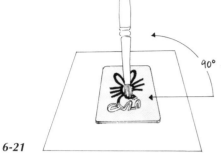

Fig. 6-21

Fig. 6-22

Using the smaller-sized Brush Pen, I was able to color the intricate design of the brass stencil (Fig. 6-22, © Judith Barker and American Traditional). You've got to admit that this little gal is an absolute doll.

POP-UPS

Pop-ups are primarily used on paper. After a print is made, cut around a portion of the outer edges of the print with a craft knife. (If you cut around all the outer edge, the print won't be a pop-up, it'll be a cut-out.)

One place where pop-ups are very effective is on the fold line of a note card. Open the card, right side of the front is up. Print over the fold line. The print will extend over to the back of the card. If you want, add color to the print with markers or embossing powders.

Keeping the card open and flat, cut along the edges of the print that are on the back of the card. Stop cutting at the fold line (Fig. 6-23). Fold the cut section forward before placing the card in the envelope. When the card is removed from the envelope, the cut section will pop up.

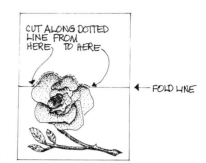

Fig. 6-23

A pop-up doesn't have to be over a folded edge; it can be used anywhere. After cutting the print, pinch the edges together, which helps it to stand up. Remember not to cut completely around the print.

You can add color to the front and back of this type of pop-up. Or you can use a print of that design on the page of the card behind the pop-up. After making the pop-up, lightly trace the cut edges on the page behind the card. Open the card. Print on top of the traced lines.

POSITIONING TOOLS

There are times when it's necessary to re-print over a colored print or to print precisely on a marking. When markers are used to color a print, the design of the print is often covered. In order for the design of a print to be visible, it's necessary to re-print with the stamp. Designs often require exact placement of prints. A design of a cow jumping over the moon loses something when the cow is plopped in the middle of the moon.

There are several positioning tools on the market. They often look like thick T or L squares. The height of the positioning tool should be at least half as high as the block. (That's why a regular ruler, T, or L square doesn't work.)

Stamp-O-Graph is a positioning tool used for non-fabric projects (Fig. 6-24). Stamp-O-Round, a positioning tool for fabric projects, holds fabric stable and taunt for exact positioning when printing and re-printing and also when coloring with markers. When this tool is used, it is not necessary to bond freezer paper to the wrong side of fabric.

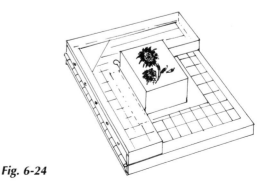

Fig. 6-24

PRINTING WITH LARGE STAMPS

If you're having problems printing with large, oversized stamps, a piece of wood or a rubber roller (brayer) will help. The wood allows you to apply even pressure to a large block; the rubber roller evenly inks the die.

The piece of wood should be about ½" thick, about 3" wide, and about 2" longer than the stamp is wide. If the piece of wood you have isn't exactly this size, don't fret. What you need is something that's longer than the longest dimension of the block (width or length).

After the stamp has been placed on the surface you are printing, put the wood piece on the back of the block. Apply pressure to the ends of the wood that extend beyond the block (Fig. 6-25). If the stamp is really big, move the wood around so that pressure is applied across the full block. Use care when you're moving the wood so that the stamp isn't moved, too. Standing at a counter also helps. You won't be tempted to squiggle the board around on the block.

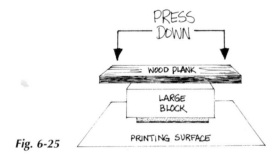

Fig. 6-25

Inking with a rubber roller (see Appendix C) is the easiest (some say the only) method for applying an even coating of ink to large dies. If you don't have a rubber roller, the die can be inked with a small cube or oval-shaped pad. Pat the pad on the die. Use the piece of wood, too. (I think that's called covering all the bases.)

PUNCHES

There are about three dozen shapes that you can punch into, or out of, surfaces. Look for punches in crafts stores and stamp stores and catalogs.

McGill Craft Punches have the familiar grip handle. The punches are available in a wide variety of shapes. They have a deep reach and wide openings. They punch Fun Foam, paper-backed fusible web, vinyl—just about any soft surface. The Utility Punches are sturdy enough to punch through magnetic sheeting.

Craft Punches by Marvy Uchida are available in more than two dozen shapes. The punches are square and made from metal. Place paper into the front slot and apply pressure to the top of the punch. As an added bonus, I use the top and bottom of the plastic box the punch comes in as a block. (Do you have visions of my digging through trash cans looking for plastic boxes to use as blocks?)

REVERSE PRINTS

This is what you do when you'd rather the dog was facing right instead of left, or two dogs are facing each other (Fig. 6-26, © Pelle's). Sometimes a company has both images of the same stamp, but that's not usually the case. Stamp stores and catalogs have "reverse stamps" (a block with a blank die). Making one is easy. Both kinds (purchased or self-made) are inked and used in the same way.

Fig. 6-26

Making a Blank Die

To make a blank die, you'll need a piece of Flex Plate (see Sax Arts and Crafts, Appendix F), a piece of Fun Foam, a wooden block, and some glue. A blank die should not be larger than 4" × 4".

Cut the Flex Plate and Fun Foam a little bigger than the top of the block you are using. Stick the adhesive side of the Flex Plate on top of the piece of Fun Foam. Glue the Fun Foam side to the top of the block. (I use marker glue.) When the glue is dry, turn the block over so the Flex Plate/Fun Foam layers are down. Use a craft knife to cut away the Flex Plate/Fun Foam that extends beyond the top of the block (Fig. 6-27).

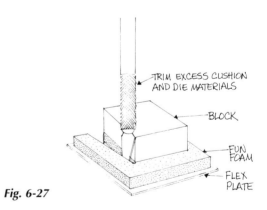

Fig. 6-27

Inking for a Reverse Print

Ink the stamp you want reversed with a pigment ink. Print on the blank die. Don't push the inked stamp down too hard, which will cause the ink to spread and smear. Check the print on the flex plate. If it's not clear, wipe it off with a damp paper towel and print again.

If the pigment ink you used was not labeled permanent, do not use it on fabric that will be laundered. Use a thick fabric paint to ink the stamp. All the other steps are the same. Pretest before beginning your project. If the paint you have selected does not transfer from the blank die to fabric, see "Transfer Ink" later in this chapter.

Printing a Reverse Print

Think of the blank die with the print described above as a stamp. When printing with this "stamp," apply more pressure to the block than you normally do. If the design is large, be sure to apply pressure over the entire block. Lift the block—there's your reverse print.

If you also want a print of the original design, don't re-ink the stamp. Print on the surface (not the blank die) with the ink that remains on the stamp. The images will be the opposite of one another; there will be little difference between the coloring of each print (see Fig. 6-26).

THERMAL EMBOSSING (EMBOSSING WITH POWDER AND HEAT)

Thermal embossing requires a slow-drying ink, embossing powder, and a heat source. Pigment and embossing inks dry very slowly. (Glues and fabric paints often work too—be sure to pretest.) Embossing powder is a microfine powder that melts with heat. An iron, hot plate, light bulb, or heat gun is used as the heat source to melt the powder.

Rules of Thermal Embossing

▶ Pretest. Inks and powders do not emboss the same on every surface or with every stamp.

▶ Use only enough ink to make a clear print. Over-inked prints become sloppy embossed prints.

▶ Use a light coating of embossing powder on the print. Too much powder makes an even bigger mess than too much ink.

▶ Remove all excess powder from the surface before applying heat. Use a soft brush if necessary. Each of those little bits that remain will melt. Once they're melted, they're there to stay.

▶ Return the excess powder back to the original container (if you are not using a flat, plastic storage container). To do this, crease the center of a piece of paper. Flatten the paper, Shake, tap, and brush excess powder onto the paper. Hold the crease over the open container and tap the back of the paper. The powder will slide down the crease into the container (Fig. 6-28).

Fig. 6-28

▶ Wipe up and remove all powders immediately from your work area (see "Things to Remember About Embossing Powders," later in this chapter).

▶ Keep containers of embossing powder out of the reach of children.

▶ Because of the flying powder and the heat required for melting it, I wouldn't recommend thermal embossing for anyone under the age of fourteen.

Inks Used for Thermal Embossing

Pigment-ink pads are available in several colors. Embossing ink is available in inked pads, fine-tip applicator bottles, markers, and pens. A substitute for an embossing pen is an erasable ballpoint pen. (Another tip from the Raindrops On Roses stamp catalog.)

Use the pen for embossed signatures. (I wonder how the bank would go for that?) Run the pen around the lines of a stencil. Use either an embossing pen or marker to "color" portions of a print or trace designs. Sprinkle embossing powder over the pen or marker lines (Fig. 6-29). Shake off the excess powder and heat.

Fig. 6-29

Embossing Ink Substitutes

In addition to glue and fabric paint, three other supplies can be used as substitutes for pigment and embossing ink. A pad can be inked with either glycerine (purchased in a drugstore) or a drying retardant (see Appendix C). Glycerine rarely dries out on a pad; a drying retardant will. Designs colored with oil pastel sticks or semisolid stencil paint can be embossed. But remember, oil pastel sticks dry faster than the other supplies mentioned.

Embossing Powders

Embossing powders come in as many colors as you could possibly imagine—from crystal clear to jet black and a couple of hundred more. Tinsel and Foil Embossing Powders are available in rich metallic colors. Combine those colors with the number of colors available in pigment inks and you've got possibilities that would require a calculator to compute. The color of pigment ink shows through or changes the color of the melted embossing powder.

Sprinkle or shake the powder over the wet ink. Some people prefer putting the powder into flat, plastic storage containers. (It has to have a tight-fitting lid.) Hold the paper upright in the container and spoon the powder over the print. The powder that didn't stick to the print will fall into the container.

Things to Remember About Embossing Powders

- The powder isn't something you'd want to eat or inhale.

- It flies all over the place, so don't use it in any area where food is prepared or eaten. If you see it floating around in your coffee cup, dump out the coffee.

- Don't try to wipe up any spills with a dry paper towel. All that does is make the stuff mad; then it really flys all over the place. Use either a damp paper towel or a Dritz Lint Pic-Up (roll it over the powder) to clean off work areas. Toss out the Pic-Up sheet or paper towel—they should not be reused.

- Store embossing powders in either tightly capped or covered containers out of the reach of children.

Heat Source

I just about burned down the house a couple of times before I got a heat gun. Talk about breaking rules—one time the hot plate was cranked up too high, and I stuck the paper right on top of it! (I have a tendency to get a little impatient.)

For occasional embossing, use an iron, hot plate, or light bulb. (A hair dryer won't work. It just doesn't get hot enough.) If you frequently emboss prints, get a heat gun. They're faster and safer. Heat guns are also an excellent substitute for an iron to heat set fabric paints.

Heat Guns

Heat guns have an open tip about 1½″ wide. They are often used to strip paint or to shrink plastic film to model bodies (airplanes and cars, as opposed to the people variety). Don't get the kind that heats up to 1,100 degrees, which is more than twice as much heat as needed for embossing powders.

Hold the tip of the gun 4″ to 6″ away from either the front or back of the surface when you're melting the powder (Fig. 6-30). Use a clothespin or wooden toast tongs to hang on to smaller items. Remember, the surface of many papers is affected by heat. If you get the gun too close, you'll end up scorching the surface (or burning down the house). Look for heat guns in stamps stores and catalogs, hobby stores and catalogs, and hardware stores.

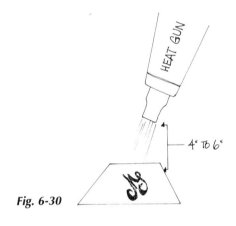

Fig. 6-30

TRANSFER INK

Although prints made with this type of ink will be reversed when transferred, the time-saving benefits far outweigh that feature. And when you print a Sun Catcher with wording, the wording will not be reversed. Another advantage is that the ink is permanent when transferred to fabric.

Prints are made on paper with transfer ink. Just about any type of paper can be used for the transferred prints. I prefer either white tissue paper or tracing vellum. Prints made on these papers transfer well, and it's handy to be able to see the surface through the paper.

Use transfer ink for "no fret" printing. After making prints, cut away excess paper around the prints. Arrange the prints faceup on projects of either paper or fabric (pretest if using wood). When you're pleased with the arrangement, turn the prints over and secure with hot tape before pressing. (Follow the ink manufacturer's instructions for iron temperature and pressing time.)

Pick up the iron when changing positions. A sliding iron creates smeared prints. Depending upon the pressure applied to the iron, you'll get at least three transfers from each print.

Although a blank die can be used for printing reverse prints (see "Reverse Prints," above), many choose to use transfer ink, especially on fabric.

If you also want a print of the original stamp, don't re-ink the stamp. Print directly on the surface while you're waiting for the first print to dry on the paper. Prints made directly on fabric with transfer ink must be heat set.

I think a "mail art jacket" would be quite a creation. Ask your mail art friends to use transfer ink. As each card arrives, transfer it to the jacket. You certainly would never have to worry about anyone having a jacket like yours. Or how about a memory quilt? Each member of the family could do a block.

WORK TABLE

With few exceptions, all printing and the folding and creasing of paper should be done on a hard surface. I sit at a tabletop covered with a large rotary cutting mat, smooth side up. It protects the top of the table from all the stainy stuff (markers, inks, glues, etc.), and it's in place when I use a rotary cutter or craft knife. The only

Fig. 6-31

time I stand at the kitchen counter is when I'm printing with large stamps. (I'd rather sit than stand any day.)

Large cutting mats can be a problem to store. If the mat is the type that can be rolled, stick it into one leg of a pair of old panty hose. Slip the elastic waistband of the hose over a hanger and hang it in the closet (Fig. 6-31). If it can't be rolled, put the mat into a pillowcase and slide it under a bed. The type with handles can be hung on a closet door or on the wall—next to the all those shelves filled with stamps and stencils.

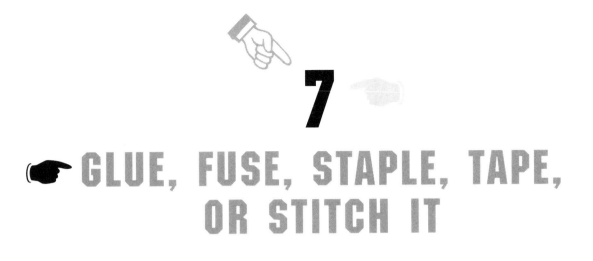

7

☞ GLUE, FUSE, STAPLE, TAPE, OR STITCH IT

We tend to limit a supply to the use it was originally intended. If it hadn't been for this book, I know I never would have considered using mounting film as a glue substitute, nor would I have played around so much with fusibles. Maybe this chapter should have been titled "Weird Ways to Use Normal Things."

GLUE IT

Making Envelopes

When you want to make an envelope, the envelope stencils from American Traditional are the way to go. They also have stencils for making gift boxes. It only takes a minute to stencil and cut out an envelope or box. Stencil one envelope and photocopy it for several envelopes or boxes. Reduce or enlarge to the size needed on a copier.

Also see the Bibliography for books that have instructions and diagrams for unusual-shaped envelopes and gift boxes. Toomuchfun Rubber Stamps has stamps for printing small envelopes and boxes.

One benefit of making your own envelopes or boxes is that it's much easier to print and emboss (thermal and pressure) a flat surface. Don't assemble an envelope or box until the decorating is completed. Use either marker glue or glue stick for speedy gluing. (Dritz plastic collar stays are a handy item to use to spread glue stick.)

A paper that is particularly nice to use for envelopes is the colored parchment paper now available in

booklets. Most crafts stores have them. Fuse metallic origami paper to the wrong side of paper used for boxes and you have instant fancy for the inside of a box.

Lining Envelopes

We can thank Sherril Watts, owner of Raindrops On Roses, for this easy method of making envelope liners. She gave permission for me to copy it from the stamp catalog.

Origami paper is probably the easiest decorated paper to use for an envelope liner. Or you can make your own decorated paper by adding either prints, or embossing powders, or glued glitter, or all of them to colored paper or tissue.

Directions

1 Cut the piece of decorated or colored paper slightly smaller than the inside of the envelope. The top of the liner should not extend over the glue line on the flap of the envelope (Fig. 7-1).

2 After cutting, put the liner back into the envelope.

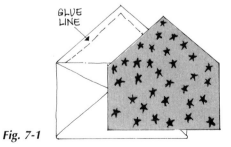

Fig. 7-1

Fig. 7-2

3 Attach the liner to the inside of the envelope with either marker glue or glue stick (Fig. 7-2).

4 If this is an envelope size you use frequently make a template of the liner from poster board or adhesive vinyl (don't remove covering from adhesive side).

Glued Beading

Bead Easy Glass Beads and Bead Easy Clear or Glitter Adhesive (see Appendix F) are the solution for a hand-beaded effect without stitching.

For a special edge on a card, empty a vial of beads into a flat container with shallow sides. (The sides of the container keep the beads from rolling all over the work table.) With a make up applicator, apply a thin line of the Glitter Adhesive to the edge of a card. Dip that edge into the beads. Press the beads into the adhesive. After the adhesive has dried, shake any loose beads from the edge back into the container. The beads can be either left in the container or returned to the vial.

FUSE IT

Just about anything that can stand a little heat can be fused. The advantages of using a fusible web, especially on paper projects, are instant bond and no glue mess.

That's the good news. The next tidbit is even better. I noticed an iron in the Tower Hobbies catalog (see Appendix E) that is used by model builders to shrink plastic film to the bodies of models. I found that not only can it be used with fusible web and iron-on transfers, it works like a charm. You can guess how much I jumped up and down—I even let out a yell they probably heard in Santa Fe.

The iron is small and has three temperature selections. The sole plate is nonstick. The tip gets into all those places a regular iron won't fit. And there's not a steam vent in sight. It's called the Top Flite MonoKote Heat Sealing Tool. (I think it should be called the Craft Iron.)

Tower Hobbies also has a teeny iron that is ideal for narrow trims and laces. That's the Top Flite MonoKote Trim Seal Tool (Craft Iron, Jr.?).

Obviously, neither of these irons are intended to be used for pressing a week's supply of shirts. But the Heat Sealing Tool is an excellent travel iron. (Save the box.) And they're both reasonably priced.

But back to using fusible web in place of glue—it's rule-breaking time. When you're fusing items that won't get laundered (paper and wood, for example), the only thing you have to worry about is the fusible web melting (so it will fuse) at a lower heat than that recommended by the manufacturer. Always follow the manufacturer's directions when fusing items that will be laundered. Because I know you *always* follow those directions, I won't bore you with my fusible web lecture.

© Ad-Lib 1993

Now don't get carried away. Even though I'm telling you to break the rules, there are only so many that can be broken. These are the unbreakable ones:

 Cover the ironing board with either white (only white) wrapping tissue paper or cooking parchment paper when using a fusible web. You can also use a Teflon pressing sheet or a Dritz pressing cloth.

 Place a piece of cooking parchment paper over fusible web that does not have a paper covering to protect the surface of the iron (Fig. 7-3).

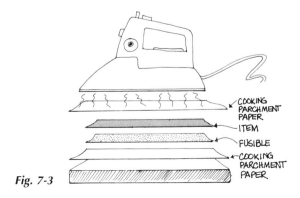

Fig. 7-3

◆ Don't disturb the fusible web (remove paper backing, remove from board, pick at the edges, etc.) until it's completely cool to the touch.

Heat n Bond (both Original No Sew and Lite) fuses when the iron is at a synthetic setting. Use Heat n Bond Original No Sew for items that will be laundered; Heat n Bond Lite for items that will not be laundered. Pretest if using another brand.

Several brands of fusible web do fuse when the iron is at a silk setting. Those fusibles can be used if surfaces will not be damaged by a higher heat or if the item will not be laundered.

To pretest if the heat required will damage a surface: Heat the iron to a synthetic setting. Cover the right side of the surface with cooking parchment paper. Leave the iron on the surface for fifteen seconds. If the surface was not affected, it can be fused with Heat n Bond.

For other brands of fusible web, use this same test with the iron set at silk. If the surface (primarily paper) buckles at that heat, cover it with cooking parchment paper, which often eliminates the problem.

When using a fusible web that requires steam, pretest without steam at a silk setting. Steam cannot be used on paper or wood.

Fusing Lace or Trims with Open Spaces to Fabric, Wood, or Paper

◆ Do not use a fusible web requiring steam.

◆ Discard white tissue paper after one use.

◆ Dritz Pressing Cloths can be used in place of the white tissue paper. Launder the cloth to remove fusible residue before using it again.

First cover the ironing board with white tissue paper. Place the lace or trim, right side down, on the tissue. Place the fusible web, fusible side down, on the wrong side of the lace or trim. Press according to the directions included with the fusible.

When cool, gently pull the tissue away from the lace or trim. If any fusible is remaining around the outer edges of the lace or trim, pull it off with your fingers.

Place the lace or trim, fused side down, on the surface (fabric, wood, or paper) you are fusing to. Cover with white tissue paper. Press; it may be necessary to push the tip of the iron in and around the edges of some trims (rickrack, for example). On paper and wood surfaces, remove the tissue paper immediately. On fabric, it can be left until cool. If any of the tissue paper sticks to the fabric, wipe it off with a wet cotton swab.

The fusible under the open spaces and around the outer edges will be absorbed by the tissue paper and will not remain on the surface.

Fusing Paper, Foil, and Mylar to Paper and Wood

◆ See "Fancy Edges" in Chapter 6.

◆ Do not use steam with foil, mylar, paper, or wood.

◆ Cover paper, foil, and mylar with cooking parchment paper or a Teflon pressing sheet. If the iron is at a synthetic setting, white wrapping tissue can be used over some papers. Pretest.

◆ It may be necessary to apply a top or finish coat over these supplies when used on wood.

Paper

Paper products include origami paper (colored, textured, and metallic), decorated wrapping papers and tissues, gift bags and boxes, drawing and sketch papers, construction papers, poster board, and bristol board. Apply fusible to lightweight paper and then fuse that paper to heavyweight paper.

Foil

Colored foil is sold by the roll and by the sheet. It's most commonly used for foil art designs on clothing. Apply fusible to a surface and then cover with foil, as described above, or apply the fusible to the uncolored side of the foil. The foil can then be fused to the surface. For best results, use Heat n Bond Lite and a synthetic setting on the iron.

After applying the fusible, a punch can be used to punch designs into the foil before removing the paper covering from the fusible. When the foil is fused to the surface, the surface will be visible in the punched-out areas. The punched-out designs also can be fused. Use the tip of a bamboo or wooden skewer to hold those little designs in place when fusing (unless you're into burned fingers).

Foil is covered with a clear film. Remove the film after fusing is completed and the foil is cool to the touch. Stick a piece of tape securely on one corner of the foil. Lift the end of the tape—off goes the film.

Mylar

Punched ribbon, wrapping paper sheets, and cut-out shapes are the most commonly found mylar products. A fusible can be applied to the back of wrapping paper sheets. Strips or shapes can then be cut with either a rotary cutter or scissors.

Making Your Own Postcards (Fusing Paper to Paper)

One speedy way to make your own postcards (for both mail art and quick notes) is to fuse 4″ × 6″ blank index cards together. The double thickness is needed for durability. Fuse Heat n Bond Lite (or a substitute) to the side of one card, using a synthetic setting on the iron. When cool, remove the paper backing on the fusible. Cover with the second card and press.

Fusing Fabric to Perforated Paper and Plastic Canvas

Perforated Paper

▶ Do not use steam with perforated paper.

▶ Perforated paper cannot be laundered.

▶ Metallic-colored perforated paper is more durable than pastel-colored paper.

Plastic Canvas

▶ Any type can be used, including the precut shapes.

▶ Any type can be laundered (cool water, line dry).

▶ The easiest to cut is the 14-count canvas used for cross stitch. It's soft and flexible.

Flat and Fold Book

I know it's a silly name, but the book can be laid out flat or folded. Children like dragging them around. They can also be folded into books. But best of all, the pages never tear.

Supplies

Muslin, 20″ × 10″ piece

Heat n Bond Original No Sew fusible web, 20″ × 18″ piece

Plastic cross stitch canvas (plastic canvas of heavier weight can be substituted), 18″ × 4½″ piece

Pad or substitute with permanent ink

Stamps the children pick out

Permanent markers

Trim, ⅛″ wide × 29″ long (¼″-wide trim can be substituted)

Directions

1 Remove selvage edges from the muslin. Wash and dry (no softeners in either wash or dry cycle). Press smooth (no spray sizing or starch).

2 Fold the muslin in half, long edges together. Steam press the fold line. Open the muslin, right side up. Fold in half, short edges together. Steam press the fold line. Fold in half again, short edges together. Steam press the fold line. Open the muslin, right side up.

3 There will be eight sections: four across the top half and four across the bottom half.

4 Print in each of the eight squares on the right side of the fabric. Color the prints with permanent markers. Heat set.

5 Fuse Heat n Bond to the wrong side of the fabric. The steamed fold lines will still be visible. Remove the backing paper from the fusible when cool.

6 Cut the plastic canvas into four 4½″ squares.

7 Lay the fabric, fusible side up, on an ironing board. Place one square of the plastic canvas in the center of each of the four squares of the bottom half.

8 Bring the top half of the fabric over to cover the tops of the plastic canvas squares. The outer edges of the fabric should be even.

9 At a synthetic setting, fuse the top half of the fabric to the plastic canvas squares. Turn over when cool. Fuse the bottom half of the fabric to the other sides of the plastic canvas squares.

10 Push the tip of the iron into the space between each piece of plastic canvas (Fig. 7-4). Do the same along the top and bottom edges.

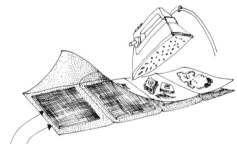

Fig. 7-4   MUSLIN WITH BONDED FUSIBLE
PLASTIC CANVAS

11 Add fusible to the wrong side of the trim.

12 Fuse the trim to the three raw edges of the fabric, following the directions in "Fusing Lace or Trims with Open Spaces to Fabric, Wood, or Paper," above.

☛ *Note: How to Make Cloth Books for Children* (see Bibliography) describes several methods you can use to make books for children.

Fused Prints

Of the two ways you can fuse prints, the first doesn't require a fusible web.

Dritz Mending Fabric, probably one of the easiest surfaces to print, is available in white and a variety of colors. Pick out the color you prefer and cover the piece with prints. Color with markers if you want. Cut out the prints and fuse them to fabric (Fig. 7-5) or wood. The heat required for fusing takes care of heat setting.

If you use fusible web, print on the fabric first. Color the prints if you want, then apply the fusible to

DECORATE AND MEND IN ONE OPERATION

Fig. 7-5

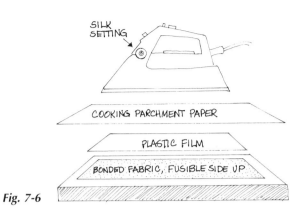

SILK SETTING

COOKING PARCHMENT PAPER

PLASTIC FILM

BONDED FABRIC, FUSIBLE SIDE UP

Fig. 7-6

the wrong side of the fabric. Cut out the prints and fuse away. Machine stitch or apply fabric paint around the edges of the appliqué if the fabric will be laundered (not required if using Heat n Bond Original No Sew).

Laminated Fabric

Laminated fabric is water-repellent and sturdy as can be. Unfortunately, it's hard to find in fabric stores, few patterns and prints are available, and it's always expensive. Fortunately, you can make your own laminated fabric from yardage you've printed.

In addition to the woven fabric, you'll need Heat n Bond Original No Sew and 2-mil plastic film. You can buy plastic film not only in a fabric store, but also in a hardware store or a lumberyard (because it's used as a drop cloth when painting). It's sold by the yard or in precut pieces. You'll need the same amount of yardage for all three supplies.

Cover the ironing board with cooking parchment paper. Leave the paper on the ironing board until all laminating is finished. Fuse Heat n Bond to the right side of the fabric. When cool, remove the backing paper. Print on the fusible. Don't use solvent-based inks; they'll dissolve the fusible. To color the prints, use permanent markers.

When the ink and markers are thoroughly dry, cover the printed side of the fabric with plastic film. Cover the plastic film with either cooking parchment paper or a Teflon pressing sheet. (Don't let the iron come in contact with the plastic film.) Press, using a silk setting on the iron (Fig. 7-6). When cool, turn over and press on the wrong side. Bingo! You now have printed laminated fabric.

Now if that seems like too much of a hassle, Heat n Bond Iron-On Flexible Vinyl laminates fabric in one step. The fusible and plastic film are already fused to one another. Prints can be made on either the right side

of the fabric, or the sticky side of Flexible Vinyl Press as directed on the label. (Double Bingo?)

Before you start stitching, do yourself (and your machine) a favor—put in a new ballpoint needle. Do some test stitches; a larger needle than what is normally used for the fabric may be needed. Place strips of white tissue paper along the seam line (between the right sides of the fabric) when stitching. Tear away when the stitching is completed. A Teflon foot makes topstitching easier.

Use laminated fabric to make a grocery bag. See Stamp Craft in Appendix G—their Fruit Collection is perfect. Refer to *The Complete Book of Machine Quilting* (see Bibliography) for instructions on how to make a flat-bottom bag.

Laminated Paper

Laminated paper is made in the same way as laminated fabric. I laminated bubble wrap to paper I had covered with fish prints. Those little fishes just bubbled with joy on the front of a card. Laminated paper prints can also be cut out and used for pins and earrings. (Laminate both sides of the paper.)

Pele Fleming, owner of Pelle's See-Thru Stamps, told me about the following laminating method. Cover a piece of 100-pound-weight bristol board with prints. Color the prints with permanent markers. Then go to a photocopier place that does laminating. One pass through their machine and it's done. After you cut out the prints you can use them for jewelry, button covers, picture frames—whatever you like.

STAPLE IT

No-Sew Christmas Tree Skirt

The first requirement for this skirt is silence. Let everyone think you spent hours and hours stitching. Just smile and accept the compliments graciously.

Once you discover how fast and easy stapling is, you'll want to do more. Be sure to read *Gail Brown's All-New Instant Interiors*. Gail has all kinds of ideas for "staple stitching."

Supplies

2⅔ yards of 54"- or 60"-wide muslin (bleached or unbleached)

☞ **Note:** You can use a white sheet to make the skirt. Cut all hems and selvage off before beginning.

One 48" Extra Special Tree Skirt Batt

Permanent fabric marker in a dark color

Straight pins

Bobby pins (extra long) or clothes pins

A dozen (or more) large safety pins

Stapler (regular size staples—the teeny, tiny ones probably won't do the job)

6 yards of trim that is at least ¾" wide (fringe is O.K. as long as band is ¾" wide)

Glue, or 6 yards of fusible web that is ¾" wide, or ¾" wide double-faced craft tape (see "Attaching the Trim," below)

Cutting the Fabric

1 Remove the selvage from the fabric either by cutting or tearing it off. Cut a small triangle from each end of the fabric. Wash and dry the fabric. Press (don't use spray starch or sizing). Cut off any loose threads. (Gladys Keller passed on this handy hint of cutting the corners on an angle before laundering—it reduces fraying to a minimum.)

2 Fold the fabric in half, short end to short end. Press the fold line with steam. Cut the fabric on the fold line. (You'll have two 1⅓-yard pieces of fabric.)

3 Fold one piece of the fabric in half, long sides together. Press the fold line with steam.

4 Fold that piece of the fabric in half again, short ends together. Press the fold line with steam. (The pressed fold lines will cross in the middle of the fabric.)

5 Place the fabric without the pressed lines on a flat surface, right side up. Smooth flat.

6 Place the fabric with the pressed lines on top of the unpressed fabric, right side down. Smooth flat. Pin the two layers together with straight pins.

7 Place the skirt batt on top of the two layers of fabric. The center opening in the batt should be centered over the crossed pressed lines in the top layer of fabric.

8 Use the marker to trace all edges (outer edges, center back, and center opening) of the batt on the fabric. Remove the batt.

9 Cut both layers of the fabric along the marked lines. Separate the fabric layers.

Printing the Skirt

1 Place the prints on the right side of one piece of the cut fabric. (Printing the right side of the second piece is optional.)

2 All prints should be at least 1" from the outer cut edge and the marked center opening and back opening.

3 In addition to prints, the fabric can also be embellished with fabric paint, sequins, beads, laces, buttons—anything you'd like included on a tree skirt.

4 Leave flat until all paint, glue, and prints are dry.

Stapling the Skirt

1 Place the unprinted piece of the fabric, wrong side up, on a flat surface. Smooth flat and cover with the batt. Place the printed piece, right side up, on top of the batt and smooth flat. The outer edges of the fabric pieces and batting should be even. Use large safety pins to hold the layers together.

2 Begin stapling at the center front edge (Fig. 7-7). (Staples should be placed ½" from all edges, closely together and almost touching.)

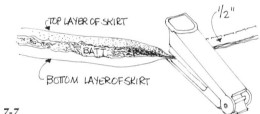

Fig. 7-7

☞ **Note:** A carpeted floor is "bouncy." If you have to staple on a floor, place cardboard under the fabric. Don't pound the top of the stapler with your fist; push down with your palm. Be sure to catch both layers of the fabric and batt.

Staple one-half of the skirt edge up to ½" from the center back opening. Then staple the other half. Staple around the edges of the center opening and back opening.

3 Trim away edges to ¼" from staples.

Attaching the Trim

1 Check to make sure you have enough trim to go around the skirt. Begin attaching trim at one edge of the center back opening. Continue around all the edges back to that end of the trim. The trim should cover the staples (or stitches, see the stitching methods, below) and extend at least ¼" beyond the outer edges of the skirt. (You want to keep the staples and cut edges a secret.)

To glue trim: Apply glue to the first 6" of the trim. Place the end of that glued piece at the center back. Secure the glued trim to the skirt with clothespins or bobby pins. (I use bobby pins—they slide off faster than clothes pins.) Continue adding glue to the trim, 6″ at a time; secure trim in place before adding glue to the next 6″ (Fig. 7-8). Dry flat. It'll probably take about three hours before the glue is stable enough to move the skirt. Leave the clothespins or bobby pins in place for six hours.

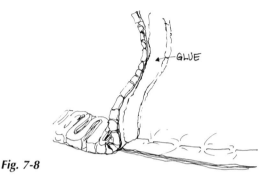

Fig. 7-8

To fuse trim: Apply fusible to the wrong side of the trim. (Fusible should not cover lower ¼″ of trim.) Use bobby pins to hold the trim along the skirt edges when fusing in place. Follow manufacturer's directions to fuse.

To use double-faced sewing/craft tape: Unroll the tape in 6″ lengths and stick it on the back of the trim. Remove the paper covering, 6″ at a time, and position the trim on the skirt. Really squash the trim into the fabric. Don't launder the skirt unless you pull off the trim. (If you stapled the skirt, it can't be laundered anyway.)

☛ *Note:* You can substitute ½″-wide cut strips of mounting film for the craft tape.

Stitching: No Turn

If you like the no-turn feature of the staple method, but aren't too keen about using staples, topstitch the edges. Follow all directions for stapling, except the actual stapling. Slide bobby pins over the cut edges to hold them together when stitching. (Remove the pins as you stitch.) Topstitch, using a medium-length stitch, ½″ from the cut edges. Trim the layers back to ¼″ from the stitched line. Add trim (see above) over the stitched line.

Stitching: Turning—The Traditional Way

The skirt can be stitched in a traditional technique (stitched right sides together, then turned right side out). Follow the directions for marking, cutting, and printing the fabric. Then press ¼″ seam allowances toward the wrong side of the fabric on all four edges of the center back.

Place the batt on a flat surface. Cover with one cut piece of the fabric, right side up. Cover with the printed piece, wrong side up. (Right sides of the fabric are together.) Smooth flat. Secure the layers with safety pins. Place under the foot of the machine so that the fabric layer is up (Fig. 7-9). Stitch (medium-length stitch) ½″ from the outer edges through all three layers. Stitch around the edge of the center hole through all three layers. Don't stitch the center back seams. Trim the stitched seams to ¼″ with pinking shears. If you don't have pinking shears, cut notches in the seam allowance every 1″ after trimming it. Stick one hand between the fabric layers and pull the batt and the layer of fabric next to the batt out through the opening (to turn the skirt right side out). Turn in the pressed seam allowances on one side of the center back; topstitch the top and bottom layers together. Repeat for the second side. Add the trim (see above) to edges.

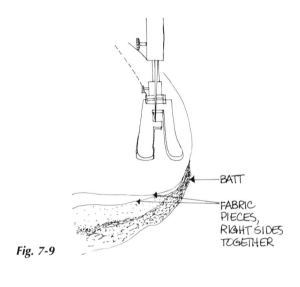

Fig. 7-9

TAPE IT

Mounting Film

Mounting film is one of the fastest supplies you can use to attach things to pin backs and button covers. Cut it out and stick it on. Double-faced sewing/craft tape doesn't have quite as much stick, but it comes in three widths. Just clip off the needed length.

Once you use mounting film or double-faced tape when glue is not an absolute necessity, you'll be spoiled.

3-D Creation

Museum of Modern Rubber came up with this method of three-dimensional construction. Double-faced sewing/craft tape reduces the time required. The creation can be used as a card, party invitation, picture frame, or conversation piece. The basic construction steps are the same for each.

Supplies

Two pieces of paper (as large as the completed size of the project and as heavy or heavier than an index card)

One piece of foam core the same size as the papers

One piece of stiff 5-mil acetate the same size as the papers

Double-faced sewing/craft tape (or mounting film or marker glue)

Permanent ink pad or substitute

Stamps of your choice (decisions, decisions)

Craft knife

Scissors

Markers or colored pencils (optional)

Directions

1 Print the design in the center of one of the pieces of paper. The design can be a single print or a grouping of prints. Set this piece of paper aside.

2 Print the same design used on the first paper in the center of the second paper. (This print will be cut out.) This paper is the top layer; decorate it as much or as little as you wish.

3 Use a craft knife to cut an X in the center of the print made in step 2. Slide the scissors into the slash and cut around the edges of the print. The paper surrounding the print should not be cut (Fig. 7-10). Place that paper on the foam core.

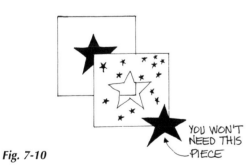

Fig. 7-10

4 Carefully trace around the inner edges of the cut-out area on the foam core. (Don't get pencil marks on the paper.) Remove the piece of paper and set it aside. The side with the tracing will be the right side of the foam core.

5 Use a craft knife to cut out the traced shape from the foam core. The cut-out section should be slightly larger than the cut-out section on the piece of paper. Set aside the cut-out piece of foam core. Use the surrounding area (the frame) in the next step.

6 Place the paper used for step 1 on a flat surface. Place the foam core frame (step 5) on top of that paper. The cut-out area of the foam core should surround (but not cover) the design printed on the paper. Place the piece of acetate over the opening in the foam core. The acetate should be about $\frac{1}{2}''$ smaller on all sides than the foam core, but it must be larger than the opening cut in step 5. If necessary, mark and cut the acetate to the right size. Replace the acetate on the foam core.

7 Place the paper that was cut (step 3) on top of the acetate, printed side up. Straighten up the edges of the bottom paper, the foam core and the top paper. Check the alignment of the four layers: The paper with the cut-out print should completely cover the foam core but not extend over the print made in step 1. The acetate should be larger than the opening in the foam core. The opening in the foam core should not extend over the print made in step 1 (Fig. 7-11).

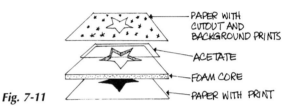

PAPER WITH CUTOUT AND BACKGROUND PRINTS

ACETATE

FOAM CORE

PAPER WITH PRINT

Fig. 7-11

8 Separate the four layers. Apply strips of sewing/craft tape around the cut opening and also along all four outer edges on both sides of the foam core. Don't remove the paper covering from the top of the tape.

9 Apply strips of sewing/craft tape around the cut opening (Fig. 7-12) and also along all four outer edges on the unprinted side of the paper that was cut. Don't remove the paper covering from the top of the tape.

10 Place the paper with the print on a flat surface, print side up. Remove the paper covering from tape on the wrong side of the foam core. Position the

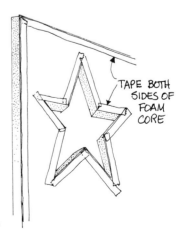

TAPE BOTH SIDES OF FOAM CORE

Fig. 7-12

foam core over the print. Remove the paper covering from the tape that is on the right side of the
foam core. Position the acetate over the tape.
Remove the paper covering from tape that is on the
cut paper. Position the paper on the acetate. That's
all there is to it.

Variations and Suggestions for Three-Dimensional Creations

▶ Add glitter, mylar shapes, or small beads to the
well before adding the acetate layer. This is a great
shaker card—just keep it away from children under
three who will figure out how to take it apart so
that they can eat the sparklies.

▶ Use the picnic basket stamp, shown 50% of original
size (Fig. 7-13, © Museum of Modern Rubber) on
the top layer for a fancy picnic invitation. Use an
invitation print with date, time, and location lines
on bottom layer. Add ants (I recommend the plastic variety—MOMR also has those in their catalog)
to the well before adding the acetate layer.

Fig. 7-13

▶ Don't use printed paper printed as the top layer;
instead glue foil, laces, buttons, ribbon, or lace on
the foam core.

▶ Cut off the Battenberg lace from a square doily.
Stiffen the lace with Fabricraft Fabric & Craft
Finish. Allow to dry. Use foam core as the top
layer. (It won't be necessary to use the top paper
layer.) Cut the foam core slightly smaller than the
lace. Attach the lace to the foam core. Use a
Victorian print for bottom paper layer. Attach the
layers to one another as directed above.

Using Stamps as Stitching and Quilting Guides

Many stamps make excellent needlework patterns. Use
transfer ink to make your own iron-on transfers.

Fig. 7-14 (Works of Heart ©) is specifically designed for embroidery stitches. Fig. 7-15 (Stuck on
Stamps © 1993) is also one of several stamps suitable
for embroidery. For a special touch, use silk thread for

© Ad-Lib 1993

Fig. 7-14

Fig. 7-15

backstitching. A bead here and there isn't a bad idea either. And don't forget, alphabet stamps and stencils are
handy to use as patterns for monograms.

Suncatchers print like a charm on counted-thread
canvas. Because you can see through the "stamp," positioning it exactly on the threads is a snap. Pelle's See-
Thru Stamps and Magna-Stamps offer the same advantage.

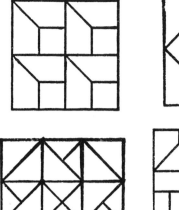

Fig. 7-16

Every quiltmaker likes to know what the finished quilt is going to look like before plunging ahead. Fortunately, there are quilt-block stamps (Fig. 7-16, © Pelle's). If the pattern you've chosen isn't available, have a stamp made.

Stamp the quilt top on plain white paper. Then fill in with colored pencils. Add lines and dots to simulate patterned fabric. When finished, frame it or keep it in your quilt notebook.

Hand or Machine Stitching
Appliqués

Prints can be used on fabric as machine- or hand-stitched appliqués. Cut prints from fabric, leaving a ⅛″ to ¼″-wide seam allowance. Fig. 7-17 (© Raindrops on Roses 1993) and Fig. 7-18 (© ImaginAir 1994) are some of the many prints suitable for stitched appliqués (see also "Fuse It," p. 71).

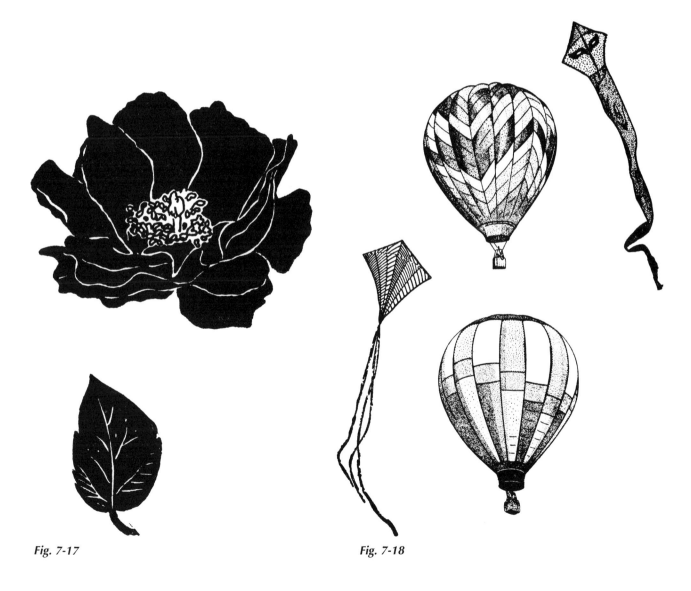

Fig. 7-17   **Fig. 7-18**

POSTSCRIPT

© Quarter Moon Rubber Stamps

By now you've found that each project leads to ideas you can use in another project. The list never ends. That's why I love the stamp in the Introduction. There are too many stamps; there isn't enough time.

As you come up with new and fantastic ideas, drop me a note and tell me about them (P.O. Box 2634, Menlo Park, California, 94026). I'd love to see what exciting things you're doing. Exchanging mail art would be fun. But it would probably be months before you got a card from me. I have an idea you'd get a little impatient waiting that long.

It would be nice if we had the chance to meet. Be sure to introduce yourself if you're at one of my workshops. I enjoy meeting my readers, and I appreciate your feedback.

One other thing—the instructions for place mats in *Fabric Painting Made Easy* (Chilton Book Company, 1993) state $\frac{1}{2}$ yard of fabric will make six place mats. You need a yard. There's absolutely no way anyone can stretch $\frac{1}{2}$ yard of fabric far enough to make six 15″ × 18″ place mats. I'm sorry if my goof caused problems.

Have a great time with instant art.

I'll leave with this question.

HAVE YOU EXERCISED YOUR PREROGATIVES TO-DAY ?

© 100 Proof Press

APPENDIX A

STAMPS

UNMOUNTED STAMPS

Unmounted stamps are not mounted (attached) to a block. Because they usually cost about half as much as mounted stamps, they are a low-cost way to feed your stamp appetite. Then there's the more practical approach—you can get two stamps for the price of one.

Depending upon the stamp company, an unmounted stamp will either be the die, which may be untrimmed, or the trimmed die already mounted on a cushion. Many companies sell sheets of cushion, either with or without adhesive and blank blocks that fit their dies. Clearsnap, Inc. sells magnetic backing kits (sheets of magnet and cushion, each with adhesive). When placed on unmounted stamps, the stamps can be used on a Magna-Stamp mount (see Chapter 1).

Trimming the Die

All you need for trimming dies and cushions is a good pair of scissors with sharp points. Small craft scissors are often used. Both Dritz and Fiskars craft scissors are available with straight and curved blades and can be purchased in sewing and crafts stores. Fiskars Soft Touch Scissors are available in two sizes. If you have problems with achy fingers or hands, they may be easier for you to use. Another type used are kitchen shears. The handles are large and the blades are sharp. The shears are found in kitchen supply stores (see Rowoco, Appendix E).

Trim the die closely, but be careful. The last thing you want to do is snip off any part of the die. (Take my word for it, those snips cannot be glued back on.)

Mounting a Trimmed Die to the Cushion

☞ **Note:** Trimmed polymer dies can be mounted directly on a plastic or Plexiglas block; a cushion is optional.

Apply mounting film to each side of the cushion if it does not have an adhesive (see "Mounting Adhesives," later, for use of rubber cement). Then follow the steps described below.

Do not remove the covering from the adhesive (or mounting film). Place the trimmed die, die side up, on a piece of cushion that is larger than the die. Trace the die on the paper covering the adhesive. Pick up the die. Place an X in the center of the tracing. Cut the cushion along the traced lines.

Place the die on the cushion again. The back of the die is on the side of the cushion with the X marking. Check the size—the cushion must be just slightly larger than the die. If the cushion is too small, you'll have to cut another cushion. A stamp will not print well when the cushion is smaller than the die.

Pick up the die. Remove the covering with the X marking from the cushion. Carefully place the die on the adhesive. It's important that the die is placed in the correct position on the cushion. Press the die securely to the cushion.

Mounting a Trimmed Die/Cushion to a Block

Remove the covering from the adhesive from the other side of the die/cushion. Center the die/cushion on the block. Apply pressure to secure the die/cushion on the block.

An excellent substitute for a sheet of cushion pur-

8 2

chased from stamp stores and catalogs is mounting tape, which is a thin foam with an adhesive layer on each side. Use the large pieces—usually found in hardware stores and used for hanging mirrors—rather than the cut strips or small squares. Follow the steps described above and in "Mounting a Trimmed Die to the Cushion."

Another substitute is Fun Foam. Don't substitute a substitute for the substitute. Fun Foam has a Westrim label on the back. Apply mounting film to both sides of the Fun Foam. Follow the steps described above for "Mounting a Trimmed Die to the Cushion."

Mounting Adhesives

The two most commonly used adhesives are rubber cement and mounting film. Remember that rubber cement is toxic and to follow all directions on the label. I prefer mounting film. When it's stuck, it's stuck. And it doesn't smell. The bad news is that it leaves a sticky residue on scissors' blades. Remove the residue with a solvent-based stamp cleaner.

RUBBER CEMENT

After trimming the die and cushion (see above), apply the cement (exactly as directed on the label) to the side of the cushion with the X marking. Position the die on the cushion. Press to secure. When dry, turn the die/cushion over and apply the cement to the back of the cushion. Center the die/cushion on the block. Apply pressure to secure the die/cushion to the block. Let dry before using.

MOUNTING FILM

There are dozens of types of mounting film on the market. The brand that is the easiest to find in both crafts and art supply stores and also is less expensive than many other brands is Grafix Double Tack Mounting Film.

Apply mounting film to each side of the cushion. After trimming the die and cushion (see above), position the trimmed die on the side of the trimmed cushion with the X marking. Remove the covering from the adhesive on the back of the die/cushion. Center the die/cushion on the block. Apply pressure to secure the die/cushion to the block.

SUBSTITUTE ADHESIVE

Mounting film and rubber cement have the greatest holding power. But Dritz Sewing/Craft Tape can be used in some cases. This double-sided tape is available in several widths. The tape may loosen with use, however, and solvent-based inks and cleaners will affect the adhesive.

I wouldn't recommend your using either marker glue or craft glue to mount unmounted stamps.

Blocks

A block should be impervious to water and stamp cleaners, so paper products of any type are out. The top of the block should be slightly larger than the cushion. When the die/cushion is mounted on the block, it should be centered on the block. Select the type of block (wood and plastic are two types) you prefer.

In addition to blocks purchased from stamp companies, found objects can also be used as blocks. Empty thread spools, cut pieces of wooden doweling, styrofoam, plastic boxes, acrylic picture frames (the type that looks like a box without a lid), jars with lids, and pieces of ⅛"- or ¼"-thick Plexiglas are some of the items that can be used (Fig. A-1).

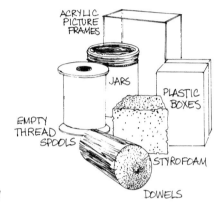

Fig. A-1

An index can be printed on the back of a wooden block with the unmounted stamp. Or the index can be printed on paper after the stamp is mounted. Secure the paper to the back of the block with heavy-duty clear tape. Be sure the index is headed in the same direction as the die. Wrong-way indexes have a way of confusing things.

Apply a sealer coat to a wood block to protect the wood and keep it from splitting. Regardless of how carefully you clean a stamp, the block will get wet.

Because I like being able to see the surface under the block, I often use some type of clear plastic as a block. Small plastic boxes with removable lids are one of my favorites. I'm out the door like a shot when acrylic picture frames go on sale. And I drive the picture framing shops crazy hounding them for scratched pieces of ⅛"- and ¼"-thick Plexiglas.

The U-shaped handle with suction cups that quilters use on plastic rulers can be used for a handle on the back of the Plexiglas (Fig. A-2). The suction cups used to hang ornaments on windows also work. Crafts and hardware stores are a good source for the large (1¾" in diameter)

Fig. A-2

size. Since they pop off and on in a snap, one handle serves many stamps. Place the suction cup (or cups, if there are two) directly over the die.

MAKING YOUR OWN STAMPS

Making your own stamps is easy. Coming up with a design may be another story. One handy item to use is Grafix Draw & Saw (purchase in art supply stores and hardware stores—the "saw" is the kind carpenters use), a clear acetate film that can be drawn, traced, and photocopied on. After a selected design has been drawn, traced, or photocopied, place the film on top of the supply used for the die and cut out the design.

Select uncomplicated designs—basic shapes are best. Dover Books has an endless supply of books with basic designs. Drawings done by children are also good to use. And don't forget my favorite—the handy, dandy cookie cutter.

There's quite a variety of supplies suitable to use for the die of stamps you make. With few exceptions, the stamps can be used for printing on any surface. But remember that all important word—pretest.

Inks and pads used for purchased stamps are also suitable for the stamps you make. When a specific type of ink (solvent-based, for example) or pad will not produce satisfactory results, it will be noted throughout the text where necessary. In some cases, pretesting is recommended. ("Recommended" really means you may be sorry if you don't.)

Generally a foam pad or substitute is the best choice for inking. The use of rubber and foam rollers is dependent upon the selected die supply. The same is true of dabber top bottles.

See "Blocks," above, for suggested supplies for blocks.

Plain water and wedge-shaped cosmetic sponges are generally the best to use for cleaning these stamps. With few exceptions, solvent-based cleaners should not be used. Those cleaners may produce adverse effects such as dissolving the die.

Supplies for Dies

Cookie cutters don't need cushions or blocks. Not only can they be used as a stamp, they also can be used as a tracing pattern on several of the supplies used for dies. Ink with either a rubber roller or foam pad (or substitute). Do not use solvent-based products, dye-based inks, washable inks, child-safe inks, markers, and felt pads. Cookie cutters should not be used with food products after using as a stamp.

Erasers are the old standby for making stamps. Those made from vinyl are the best to use. Very often the words "fabric eraser" or "carving block" will be on the eraser. Factis Extra Soft Erasers are the easiest to cut. Don't use

the yellow erasers imbued with a cleaner because they won't print.

To transfer a design to an eraser, draw (or trace) the design on typing paper (not the erasable or correctable types) with a soft lead pencil. Use the pencil to color in the portions of the design that you want to print. Place the design face down on top of the eraser. Rub hard across the back of the paper with your finger to transfer the pencil markings on the paper to the top of the eraser (Fig. A-3). Remove the paper.

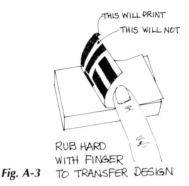

Fig. A-3

With a small craft knife, cut away the unmarked portions of the eraser. What is cut away will not print; what is left will print. Downward cuts should be perpendicular to the top of the eraser and at least ⅛" deep. Cuts made across the eraser should be parallel to the top of the eraser (Fig. A-4). After cutting, brush away loose bits and pieces from between the cuts.

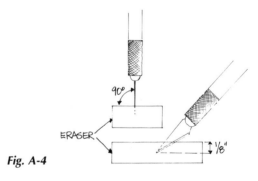

Fig. A-4

Clean ink from the eraser with a damp wedge-shaped cosmetic sponge. Don't scrub—chances are you'll tear off pieces of the design. Do not use solvent-based products. Pretest dye-based inks, washable inks, child-safe inks, markers, and felt pads.

Friendly Plastic Work Mat is made from red rubber. Use either a cushion purchased from a stamp store, Fun Foam, or mounting tape. Mount with either sewing/craft tape or mounting film. Pretest felt pads.

Fun Foam is easy to use (see "Mounting a Trimmed Die/Cushion to a Block," above). Mount with either marker glue, sewing/craft tape, permanent craft glue, mounting tape, or mounting film. Do not use with solvent-based products or markers. Pretest dye-based inks, washable inks, child-safe inks, and felt pads.

Hot glue gun pads are a translucent polymer material and are available in two thicknesses. (Look for them in the hot glue gun display in a crafts store.) If a cushion is desired, use either Fun Foam or mounting tape. Mount with either sewing/craft tape or mounting film. Pretest markers. Do not use felt pads.

Pen Score (see Appendix F) is made from a special foam that offers unique options. Pen Score is available in precut shapes and sheets. The shapes are approximately ¾" thick; the sheets are ¼" thick. After heating, impressions can be made on the softened foam (follow the manufacturer's instructions). The precut shapes do not need a block. The sheets cut easily with scissors and can be mounted with either glue stick, sewing/craft tape, or mounting film. Do not use with solvent-based products. Pretest markers and felt pads.

Design A Stamp is an easy-to-use supply for making your own dies. Designs can be traced or drawn with pencil or marker on the soft foam surface that cuts easily with scissors. The adhesive backing sticks firmly to every type of block except styrofoam. Design A Stamp is available by the sheet or in kits that include wood blocks. Do not use with solvent-based products. Pretest dye-based inks, washable inks, child-safe inks, markers and felt pads.

Sun Catchers (see description in Chapter 1) are available in a variety of sizes and designs. Purchase those with a solid back. I included them in this section because a handle or block must be added. Either suction cups used on windows or those on the plastic rulers used by quilters are the easiest to use as a handle. They also can be mounted on acrylic picture frames with mounting tape or mounting film. Do not use solvent-based products, dye-based inks, washable inks, child-safe inks, markers, and felt pads.

Flex Plate (see Appendix F) is probably the fastest supply to use. It has one adhesive side and cuts easily with scissors. Use two or more layers, or mounting tape, if you prefer. Do not use with solvent-based products. Pretest dye-based inks, washable inks, child-safe inks, markers, and felt pads.

Making Roller Stamps

The best supply for the die is Fun Foam, Flex Plate, or Design A Stamp. Use either a Dritz Lint Pic Up handle, a rubber roller, a wall paper seamer, or an old rolling pin for the roller.

Punch out shapes from either of the supplies mentioned for the die with McGill Punches. Use either a rotary cutter or scissors for cutting larger shapes or strips. Flex Plate and Design A Stamp need no adhesive for mounting on the roller. Fun Foam can be mounted on the adhesive roller of a Dritz Lint Pic-Up (Fig. A-5) with mounting tape or mounting film on the other rollers. Do

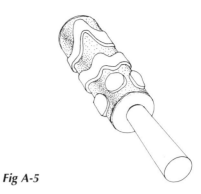

Fig A-5

not use solvent-based products. Pretest dye-based inks, washable inks, child-safe inks, markers and felt pads.

Sponge Stamps

These include precut shapes and those you cut from sheets of compressed sponge. If making your own, remember to trace and cut out the design before expanding the compressed sponge. One dip in water and that wafer-thin sponge pops up to a ¾" thickness. (Wet fingers, hands, and countertops also expand the sponge.)

I mount both types of sponge stamps on styrofoam blocks. Inking and printing are much easier when a sponge stamp is on a block. And the block keeps my fingers and hands clean.

MAKING A BLOCK FOR A SPONGE STAMP

To make the block, cut a piece of styrofoam (½" to 1" thick) slightly larger than the sponge stamp. Make it easy—cut straight-sided blocks (squares, rectangles, etc.), regardless of the shape of the stamp. Coat all sides of the styrofoam with dimensional fabric paint or permanent glue. Allow to dry. This coating keeps the styrofoam from shredding during use. (Coating the block with glue is optional, but I recommended doing it.)

If stamp is made from compressed sponge, trace and cut out the design. Expand the sponge with water.

MOUNTING A SPONGE STAMP

Apply a liberal coat of the glue used on the styrofoam block to the back of the sponge stamp. Allow to dry.

Apply a second coat of the glue to the back of the stamp. Press the stamp on the top of the block. Allow to dry.

INKING A SPONGE STAMP

The secret of getting a good print with any type of sponge stamp is to have a thin layer of ink. First wet the stamp thoroughly. Push it against the side of the sink to remove excess water. Then place it on two or three thicknesses of paper towels and push on the back of the block to remove as much moisture as possible.

The stamp can be inked in one of three ways: pat the stamp on an inked foam pad (the newer the better); ink

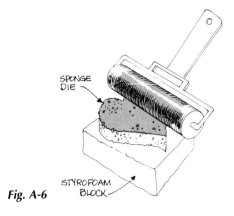

Fig. A-6

with a rubber roller (Fig. A-6); or pat the stamp on an inked freezer paper "pad" (see Appendix C). Inking on a freezer pad is usually the best method to use when printing on fabric. Do not use solvent-based inks on sponge stamps. To clean ink from the stamp, rinse under running water.

PRINTING WITH A SPONGE STAMP

Place your fingers on the back of the block. Press on the block so that the sponge is flattened on the surface. Fig. A-7 is a print made this way. The stamp was inked with a rubber roller. For a mottled effect (see "Background Prints" in Chapter 6), an inked stamp is lightly tapped on the surface. A second color can be tapped over the first if desired.

Fig. A-7

STORING STAMPS

Buying and making stamps is fun. Figuring out where to store them is another story. It's important that stamps aren't stored in direct sunlight or in very hot or cold spots. Don't store them in plastic boxes with tight-fitting lids or in plastic bags. You could end up with a mess of moldy stamps.

I think it's better not to store stamps on the die. My suggestion is to store them either on the back or side of the block. If kept in storage containers (boxes, baskets, drawers, etc.), label the containers with the type of stamp inside (e.g., bunnies, holidays, quilt blocks). These labels save a lot of searching. To save space, use shallow storage containers. (Keep bottles of fabric paint and glue in deep containers.)

Look for plastic baskets and cardboard boxes that will slide into the slots of letter files (the plastic type used in offices). The catalog from Pelle's See-Thru Stamps includes a description of the type of cardboard box that can be used with letter files. If you're not able to get them locally, you can order them from the catalog. Letter files can be stacked up to twelve high on uncarpeted floors.

By the way, letter files are also the best storage spot for the papers you use in stamping. Just slide them into the slot. The papers stay nice and flat. And one glance tells you what you have on hand.

Watch the classified ads for cabinets being sold by drafting and architectural firms or picture framing stores. They use cabinets with shallow drawers. You might be able to pick up some bargains when they replace their equipment.

Units of plastic drawers supported in plastic frames can be purchased in variety/discount stores. At least two brands have units with shallow drawers.

An out-of-the-way storage system is the wire rack storage units that are hung on doors. Look for the kind with coated shelves that are at least 4" deep.

Then there's all that empty wall space you've got. Show off your stamp and brass stencil collection on wall-hung shelves.

STAMP DIRECTORY

The labels on storage containers tell you what's inside. It's also handy having a print of each stamp you have. Get an inexpensive picture album with plastic sleeves. Each time you buy a stamp, make a print of it on a blank index card; use computer or typing paper for large stamps. If the stamp has inking peculiarities (some do), note that on the back of the card or paper. Stick the mask for the stamp (see Chapter 6) on the back if you don't like storing it on the block. Slide the card or paper into the sleeve, print side out.

And the next time someone pulls out pictures from their vacation, pull out your stamp directory.

APPENDIX B

INKS

INK BASICS

Most fluid or semifluid products can be used as an ink. In order for a product to be a suitable ink, it must be fluid enough to be applied (inked) on the die and then released (printed) onto another surface. Traditional inks are products intended specifically for stamping and are available in either inked pads, dabber bottles, or re-inker bottles. Nontraditional inks are products not generally intended for stamping and are rarely available in either inked pads or dabber bottles.

Always select an ink or marker suitable for the surface being printed. How the project will be used also determines the type of ink required. Consult the label for information concerning the use and properties of a product. Embossing inks (pads, markers, and pens) dry very slowly and are used only with embossing powders. Inks labeled "dye-based" are not permanent unless coated with a permanent finish. Be sure to pretest. Inks labeled "pigment" dry slowly and are either nonpermanent or permanent, depending upon the brand. Transfer inks are permanent after being transferred with heat to porous surfaces (paper, fabric, wood). Leather paints can often be used on several surfaces, including plastic.

Glass stain can be substituted for glass paint, but these products are not permanent on fabric. Spray paints, including glitter type, are either permanent or nonpermanent (consult the label).

Inks (including solvent-based products, acrylic fabric and craft paints, glues, etc.) labeled either "permanent when dry" or "waterproof" can be used on several surfaces—consult the label. Inks labeled "dye-based," "washable," or "child-safe" rarely print well on nonporous surfaces. Heat-set inks (including markers) can be used on fabric that will be laundered, unless the label specifies otherwise. Test prints save time and disappointment. As much as possible, test prints should be made on a surface similar to the one used for a project.

NONPERMANENT INKS (TRADITIONAL AND NONTRADITIONAL)

Dye-based Inks

Dye-based inks, either in pads or re-inker bottles, do not have the permanent properties of either a fabric dye or fabric paint labeled a dye. Dye-based inks are not permanent on any surface.

To learn if an ink is dye-based, print on scrap paper and let dry. Rub a damp cotton swab over the print. If it smears, or the color rubs off on the swab, the ink is dye-based.

Apply a protective finish to dye-based inks on porous surfaces; spraying may be necessary.

Pigment inks—most brands are not permanent on fabric (consult the label).

Watercolor markers—these are not permanent on any surface. A protective finish is required for permanency.

Craft paints—consult the label for permanent properties. Not all types are permanent.

PERMANENT INKS (TRADITIONAL AND NONTRADITIONAL)

Permanent Fabric Markers

When using permanent markers on fabric, it is recommended to bond freezer paper to the wrong side of the fabric and use an antifusant. Heat setting is required if fabrics will be laundered.

Testors Gloss Paint Markers

This brand of marker contains opaque enamel paint. They are excellent for use as an ink and also for coloring prints on items that receive heavy use (canvas rugs, cloth shoes, jean jackets, and banners or wind socks that are hung out-of-doors, etc.). It is not necessary to use an antifusant.

Do not allow marker to dry on the die. Clean stamps immediately after printing, using either a turpentine substitute or solvent-based stamp cleaner. Remove cleaners from the die and block with a damp sponge, then dry the die and block. Ink the stamp on a glycerine inked pad. Stamp on paper towels to remove glycerine from the die.

Acrylic Fabric Paint in Dabber Bottle

The only acrylic fabric paint in a dabber bottle available at this time is Fabra-Ca-Dabra (see Appendix F). Heat setting is required when used on fabric. In most cases, this product can be used when permanent ink is listed as a supply. Pretest and follow the directions on the label.

Solvent-based Inks

Two types of these products are available, those labeled "fabric" and those labeled "for plastic." Depending upon the brand, they are available in either inked pads, re-inker bottles, or dabber top bottles. Solvent-based cleaners are required for cleaning the stamps.

Solvent-based ink for fabric is suitable for most porous surfaces. Ink is permanent when dry; heat setting is not required. Solvent-based ink for plastic is suitable for most nonporous surfaces. Consult the label for suggested surfaces.

Transfer Inks

Transfer ink is available in inked pads and re-inker bottles. It can be used directly on fabric; heat setting is required for permanency (see "Transfer Ink" in Chapter 6).

Pigment Inks

The Imprintz brand of pigment ink is permanent on fabric; heat setting is required. Consult the labels of other brands (see "Nonpermanent Inks," above).

Craft Paints

☛ **Note:** Use of these products may require your inking a pad or substitute. Some craft paints dry very quickly. Clean the stamps immediately after use. Check the inked pads frequently and rinse the pad clean as soon as the paint appears dry.

Craft paints are suitable for a variety of surfaces. A textile medium is usually required when used on fabric. Consult the label.

See "Stamping on Plastics" in Chapter 5 for suggested craft paints for use on plastic.

SEALERS AND PROTECTIVE FINISHES

Jo Sonja's All Purpose Sealer can be used as both a sealer and protective finish on several surfaces. Consult the label.

Several brands of craft paint also have sealer and finish products. Consult the label for suitable surfaces and use.

Glues

☛ **Note:** Use of these products requires your inking a pad or substitute. Clean the stamp immediately after use. Do not store pads inked with glue. Rinse glue from the pad immediately after use.

Glue has to stay on top of the surface in order to get a good print. The thicker, the better when it comes to using glue on fabric. Either inking the die with a rubber roller or patting the die on an inked freezer paper "pad" (see Appendix C) is usually the best method of inking with glue.

Texture Paste

Jo Sonja's Texture Paste is suitable for porous surfaces that will not be laundered and most nonporous surfaces. Ink the die with a rubber roller (see Appendix C). Pretesting is recommended. Before printing, remove the Texture Paste from the block or cushion with a cotton swab or Wipe-Out Tool. The Texture Paste can be tinted with Jo Sonja's Artist Colors. Consult the label for additional information.

Fabric Paints

☛ **Note:** Use of these products requires your inking a pad or substitute.

New products are constantly being introduced by fabric paint companies. Don't limit your selection to those mentioned. In most cases, fabric paint can be used successfully on any porous surface (consult the label for surfaces suitable for the paint you have selected). Select a paint with the properties needed for the desired effect (for example, an opaque paint is necessary when printing on dark denim).

OPAQUE COLORS

If the label on the fabric paint bottle states that two coats may be needed for complete coverage, the paint probably will not leave a clear print on darker fabrics, particularly denim. Pretest before beginning your project. In many cases, results are improved if either a Petifour or cosmetic wedge is used as a pad for inking.

Brands that cover denim with one coat include Dizzle Brights, Jacquard Opaque, Createx Opaque, Jo

Sonja's Artist Colors (mix with Jo Sonja's Textile Medium), and Setacolor Opaque (a Pebeo product).

METALLIC COLORS

Several brands of metallic paint print well on light-colored fabrics. Some may not leave a clear metallic print on dark-colored fabric. Pretest before beginning your project. In many cases, results are improved if either a Petifour or cosmetic wedge (see Appendix C) is used as a pad.

Brands that print well on dark fabrics include DecoArt SoSoft Metallics; Dizzle Brights; Tulip Soft Metallics; Jacquard Metallic Colors; Neopaque Metallic Colors; Setacolor Opaque Metallic Colors; Jo Sonja's Artist Colors Rich Gold, Micacious Pigment (mix with Jo Sonja's Textile Medium); Setacolor Opaque Gold and Testors Gloss Paint Marker.

SUN PRINTING (HELIOGRAPHIC) PAINT

To my knowledge, Setacolor Transparent (see Pebeo, Appendix E) is the only brand of fabric paint that can be used for sun printing. Setacolor Transparent can be used directly from the bottle as an ink, but it must be diluted with water for sun printing. When a mask (see "Masking" in Chapter 6) is placed on wet paint or prints, the masked area will be a lighter shade than the unmasked areas after exposure to sunlight.

MARBLING PAINT AND AIRBRUSH INKS

These types of fabric paint are usually excellent inks. They are thinner than most other types, so it's easier to saturate a pad evenly.

Marbling or airbrush ink brands include DEKA, Createx, Versatex, and Pebeo. Delta Fabric Dye, Tulip Brush Top, and Duncan Scribbles can be diluted to the consistency of marbling paint. Foam pads inked with Pebeo Marbling Paint stay moist for weeks if kept in a airtight bag in the refrigerator.

PUFF PAINTS

Follow the paint manufacturer's instructions when applying heat to puff paint. Hand washing and line drying are often required.

Ink stamps with a rubber roller (see Appendix C). Check the die to make sure there is an even layer of ink.

T-shirt knit has a tendency to pucker up when the paint is puffed. Bond freezer paper to the wrong side of the fabric before printing or painting with puff paints. Don't remove the paper until after the paint has been puffed. The paper holds the fabric taut so that the shirt doesn't shrivel up like a prune.

Marvy Uchida Liquid Appliqué is a puff paint in a small barrel tube. Apply from the tip to outline prints. Remove the tip (turn clockwise) when inking a pad or when paint is used to ink a rubber roller. (It'll come out of the barrel twice as fast with the tip removed.) This product can be used on paper and wood, in addition to fabric.

Pebeo Puff Paste is an additive used with Setacolor Opaque and Transparent Fabric Paints (also Pebeo products). Createx Puff is an additive used with Createx Textile Colors. Both of these puff additives really puff. Follow the directions on the bottle when mixing the paint and additive. Dry for at least one week before laundering; launder as directed on the label.

Transparent Tints

This is the type of paint often used for painting preshaded iron-on transfers; the colors of the transfer are visible through the paint. A stamp print is also visible through the paint.

There are several brands of premixed transparent tints; other brands require the use of an additive (DecoArt and Palmer, for example). Additives can be found next to the brand's fabric paint. Don't mix additives of one brand with paints of another brand.

Transparent tints can be used as a protective finish over prints made with permanent and nonpermanent pigment ink. To guarantee satisfactory results if the project is to be laundered, launder the test print before proceeding with your project.

After the print is dry, heat set on the wrong side of the fabric. (Cover the fabric with cooking parchment paper or a Teflon pressing sheet and press with a dry iron at the cotton setting.)

When the fabric has cooled, use a soft brush to apply a thin coat of a transparent fabric paint over the print. Prints made with nonpermanent inks must be completely covered with paint (what isn't covered washes out in the first wash). Follow heat setting and laundry instructions on the paint bottle (also see "Protective Finishes and Glazes for Prints," later in this appendix).

GLITTER PAINTS

Glitter paints cannot be used as an ink because they do not release from the die. However, they can be used to outline or enhance prints on porous surfaces. Some glitter paints are not permanent. Read the label before use.

SPRAY FABRIC PAINTS

It's no surprise that these paints cannot be used as an ink. Instead, they can be used to enhance a printed design on porous surfaces (see "Background Prints" in Chapter 6).

MAKING YOUR OWN FABRIC PAINT

Making your own fabric paint isn't as difficult as you may think. Createx (see Appendix E) has everything first-time paint makers need from binders to textile mediums to ultrafine glitter to liquid pigments (and advice).

OTHER PRODUCTS USED ON FABRIC

☛ **Note:** Use of these products requires your inking a pad or substitute.

Antifusant

An antifusant is a starchlike liquid brushed on the fabric and dried before coloring prints with markers. Taking the time to apply an antifusant is time well spent. It completely eliminates the hassle of "marker run" on fabric.

Jacquard No Flow and Pebeo Silk Anti Difusant rinse out of fabric completely after markers or ink have been heat set.

Resist

Clear resist is applied wherever you do not want paint. Think of it as a liquid mask. Saturate a foam pad with resist. Ink the stamp and print.

Allow resist to dry before painting or printing with ink on the fabric. After paint or prints are dry, heat set. Rinse the fabric in water, following the directions on the resist bottle. A print made with resist will be the original color of the fabric (Fig. B-1).

Protective Finishes and Glazes

After the print is dry, heat set. Then apply a light coat of the finish over the print. Brands of protective finishes include Aleene's Transfer It, Delta Naplique, Fabricraft Fabric & Craft Finish, Fabricraft Solutions, Galacraft

RESIST PRINT

Fig. B-1

Magic Transfer Medium, and Plaid Sealer for Press & Peel Foil.

If you're dying to finish a project and haven't a drop of protective finish in the house, a light coat of either diluted (if brand allows) or thin-bodied permanent fabric glue that dries clear can be brushed over the print (also see "Transparent Tints," above).

APPENDIX C

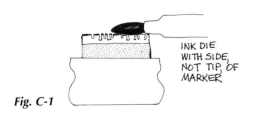 # PADS

PAD BASICS

Solvent-based inks must be used on a felt pad; water-based inks can be used on either a felt or foam pad. Because felt pads are hard, a stamp is usually pushed lightly on the surface of the pad. For foam pads, which are softer than felt, a stamp is usually tapped lightly on the surface of the pad. Foam pads can also be patted lightly on the die. Self-inked pads require proper storage to keep the ink from drying out. Rinse water-based inks from self-inked pads and substitutes (foam, latex, sponge) with plain water.

INKERS

Markers

An inker is anything used to apply ink to a die. Markers are probably the handiest inkers available. Wipe or roll the side of the tip across the surface of the die (Fig. C-1). Using the point of the tip can break it down to a fuzz ball.

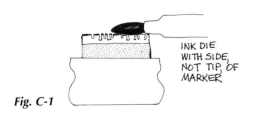

INK DIE WITH SIDE, NOT TIP, OF MARKER

Fig. C-1

Dabber-type Bottles

The top of these bottles inks a stamp almost as quickly as a marker—just wipe or dab it on the die. Remember to do

a few test prints before beginning your project. Not every dabber top or ink produces the same result with every die.

HOW TO INK PADS

It's important the layer of ink on a pad is even. Ideally the entire pad should be saturated with ink. At the very least, the ink should completely cover the top of the pad. Usually the easiest way to spread ink evenly over a pad is with a wide brush used for fabric painting (Fig. C-2). Very thin inks (watercolors, calligraphy inks, drawing inks, etc.) can be applied to the pad with an eye dropper.

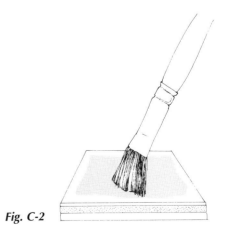

Fig. C-2

After coating the top of the pad, push the ink into the pad with the back of a plastic spoon (Fig. C-3), an expired charge card, or a rubber roller. It may be necessary to re-peat these steps with thicker inks (certain types of fabric

Fig. C-3

paint, for example). A saturated pad produces better prints and won't dry out as quickly as one that is lightly inked.

Drying retardant helps slow the drying process of acrylic craft and fabric paints. Ink the pad with a thin layer of the retardant before applying the paints to the pad. Not all companies have a drying retardant to use with their products. Don't combine brands. Products of one brand may not be compatible with products of another brand.

MAKING A FELT PAD

This is really the only pad you can make. Water-based inks can be rinsed from this pad, solvent-based inks cannot. See "Substitute Pads and Inkers" (below) for a discussion on products and supplies that can be used in place of a purchased pad.

Cut two or three pieces (3" × 5" is a good size) of either tightly needled batting or felt. Fuse the layers of batting or felt together with a lightweight fusible. Fuse a piece of muslin over the top of the pad. (Dritz Mending Fabric can be used as a substitute for the muslin.) The woven fabric holds the fuzzies down (Fig. C-4).

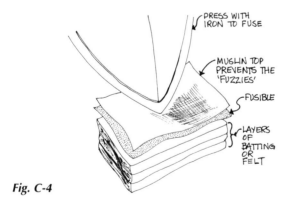

PRESS WITH
IRON TO FUSE

MUSLIN TOP
PREVENTS THE
'FUZZIES'

FUSIBLE

LAYERS
OF
BATTING
OR
FELT

Fig. C-4

SUBSTITUTE PADS AND INKERS

The following products and supplies can be used in place of purchased ink pads. Refer to Appendix F for sources of supplies.

Heavy-duty Felt Gard

Felt Gards are made of dense polyester/latex felt with an adhesive side and are placed on the bottom of furniture to protect wood floors. In addition, they are an outstanding

substitute for a felt pad. Felt Gard is available in packs of cut circles (ranging up to 1½" in diameter) or rectangular pieces (4½" × 6"). The circles are perfect when you need a small pad. Attach them to plastic boxes or empty thread spools.

Water-based inks can be rinsed from this felt with water. Follow the same procedure used when cleaning self-inked foam pads (see "Cleaning Self-inked Pads," later in this chapter). Solvent-based inks cannot be rinsed out.

Contact the company (see Felt Gard, Appendix E) if you're not able to find them in a local hardware store.

Freezer Paper

Some thick inks work best when rolled out in a thin layer on a nonporous surface with either a hard or soft rubber roller (do not use a foam roller). Put a piece of freezer paper, shiny side up, on your kitchen counter and roll away (Fig. C-5).

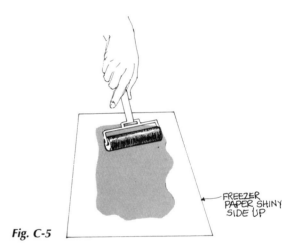

FREEZER
PAPER SHINY
SIDE UP

Fig. C-5

Lightly tap the stamp on the ink layer on the freezer paper. Be sure the die has an even layer of ink. Clean off any ink that got on the block or cushion with a cotton swab or a Wipe-Out Tool before printing.

You'll notice that the roller also was inked as you rolled the ink over the freezer paper. See "Rubber Rollers" (below) and "Foam Rollers" (later in this chapter) for directions on how to use a roller to ink a stamp.

Rubber Rollers (Brayers)

Select either a hard or soft rubber roller. The rollers can be inked on freezer paper (see "Freezer Paper," above) and on an inked pad. If inking on freezer paper, the coating of ink on the roller should be even with no globs, hunks, or bare spaces here and there. To use an inked pad, run the roller back and forth over the pad—don't use a pad that's as dry as a bone).

Place the stamp, die up, on a flat surface. Roll the ink over the die. Keep the roller as flat as possible on the surface of the die. Any area that's inked will shine. Check the die and re-ink areas that are dull. Wipe off any ink that got on either the cushion or block with a cotton swab or Wipe-Out Tool.

A rubber roller may be the inking solution for those stamps that simply refuse to print clearly. Inking with a roller also is the easier way to ink large stamps. Rubber rollers can be purchased in crafts and art supply stores and catalogs. Look for brayers—that's the official name.

Real Latex Foam Rubber Sheets

This product equals the quality of a purchased dry foam pad. It's available in 9″ × 12″ sheets, in a ¼″ thickness. This foam is used by model builders to protect radio equipment from vibration. (If it works, who cares what it is, right?)

If not available in local hobby stores, order from Tower Hobbies (see Appendix E).

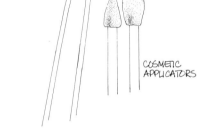

COMPUTER SWABS

PETIFOUR

COSMETIC APPLICATORS

Computer Cleaning Swabs

Computer stores have foam swabs in ⅛″- and ¼″-sized tips. Either size can be used to roll ink over a stamp. The small size is excellent for dabbing ink on a stamp.

Wedge-shaped Cosmetic Sponges

This is one of my can't-get-along-without-it stamping supplies. Look for them in drug and grocery stores. I haven't found any differences between foam or latex. Look for those with smoothly cut tops and sides. The wedges are excellent (superior, really) inkers that can be used with just about any type of ink. Use for pretesting non/traditional inks when making only a few prints, and as a small pad.

To ink a cosmetic wedge, squirt a small amount of ink on a piece of freezer paper or plastic food wrap. Tap the wide end of the wedge in the ink until the end is saturated. If the ink appears to be very thick on the end of the wedge, stamp the excess on scrap paper. Then tap or pat the wedge on the die. The wide end of the wedge can also be inked by tapping it on the surface of an inked

pad. (A juicy one gives the best results.) Use the narrow end to dab ink on portions of a die. This end is flexible and can be used as a paintbrush.

More uses for the handy, reusable wedge are found in Chapters 2 and 6.

Round Cosmetic Sponges

These sponges are often labeled "latex foam." Get the thickest ones you can find. I think round sponges are easier to use if they're mounted on a block (such as wood, the covers from small plastic boxes, ⅛″ Plexiglas, etc.). Apply a coat of glue to the back of the sponge. (Marker glue is the easiest to use.) Place the block on the wet glue immediately. Push down on the block to secure it to the sponge. Let the glue dry completely before inking the sponge. Purchase cosmetic sponges at drug and grocery stores.

Petifours

These small square sponges are an excellent substitute for a foam pad. Ink them the same way as you would a cosmetic wedge (see above). The wing-shaped pieces on the back keep your fingers clean.

Foam Cosmetic Applicators

That small piece of foam attached to the end of a small strip of plastic or stiff paper is what makes foam cosmetic applicators so handy. Dip the applicator tip into very thin inks (watercolors, calligraphy inks, drawing inks, etc.), and use it like a marker. The applicators are an excellent substitute for a small brush. Purchase cosmetic applicators at drug and grocery stores.

Disposable Foam Brushes

All widths of disposable foam brushes can be used. Look for the bags containing one handle and six brush tips; they're usually cheaper than six individual brushes.

Foam Rollers

Apply ink to a foam roller as described in "Freezer Paper" (see above). The roller works best if it's saturated with ink. Roll the roller over the die without applying too much pressure. As soon as you start pushing the roller down on the die, ink squirts all over the place. Clean off any ink that gets on the block with a cotton swab or a Wipe-Out Tool.

When you want the background to have a sponged effect, ink a dry foam roller by rolling it over an inked foam pad (a juicy pad—no dried out, dead ones). Only the surface of the roller should be inked. Use a gentle touch when inking the roller. Areas receiving more ink will print darker.

The key to satisfactory results is consistent pressure when printing. It's easy to apply too much pressure on the foam roller. Purchase the rollers in crafts (look in the DecoArt Fabric Paint display) and art supply stores and catalogs.

STORING INKED PADS AND SUBSTITUTES

Purchased Inked Pads

Purchased inked pads do not dry out quickly because you can close the top of the case to preserve them.

When the pad appears dry, turn the case upside down. (I always store my pads upside down.) Ink from the bottom of the pad will seep to the top. If the pad is still dry after twelve hours, it's time to re-ink or buy a new pad.

If it seems that you're going through a lot of pads, the problem may be that you're using only the center of the pad to ink a stamp. Use the edges of the pad whenever possible—with smaller stamps, for example.

Self-inked Pads and Substitutes

Inks that are not traditional stamping inks (acrylic craft and fabric paints, glues, etc.) dry out quickly on the pad. Of the inks I use, Pebeo Marbling Paint is the slowest drying. When properly stored, a foam pad (purchased and substitutes) will stay moist at least two weeks. I've had pads that were still moist after six weeks.

Pads you ink with nontraditional inks must be kept in a tightly closed (zipped is best) plastic bag in the refrigerator. Be sure to label each one with the date and the type of ink.

I put the plastic bags into a plastic food container with a snap-close cover. I got tired of trying to figure out if I had a refrigerator full of stamp pads or leftovers.

CLEANING SELF-INKED PADS

Check a pad at least every three days. Some inks dry out quickly, especially if the pad was not saturated with ink. As soon as the ink appears to be drying out, rinse the ink from the pad with plain water. Never use soap or detergent, which can take hours of rinsing to get out. If necessary, soak the pad in water.

If an acrylic paint dries completely, don't waste your time trying to get it out of a pad. Acrylic paints are absolutely permanent when dry.

Squeeze—don't twist—the pad when rinsing out the ink. When all ink is removed, put the pad between layers of towels. Push down on the towels to remove excess water from the pad. Dry the pad flat. Allow to dry before re-inking.

APPENDIX D

☞ PAPERS

Below are brief descriptions of the papers most commonly used for stamped projects. Generally, the papers are available in crafts and art supply stores. Also see the Arts and Crafts Supplies catalogs listed in Appendix F.

Blank stationery, note cards, greeting cards, envelopes, stickers, gift tags, boxes, and bookmarks are available in crafts, art supply, office supply, stationery, and stamp stores. Several stamp catalogs also carry blank paper supplies.

Artist Sketch Tablets and **Artist Sketch Vellum** are available in tablets and blank books. The papers are low cost and suitable for many stamping projects.

Bristol Board (100-Pound) is sold in tablets and by the sheet. The weight of this paper is excellent for greeting cards and boxes. Bristol board is available with either a vellum or smooth surface. A smooth surface has a low-gloss finish; a vellum surface is slightly more absorbent.

Card Stock is usually available in sheets. This paper is slightly heavier than an index card.

Colored Parchment Paper is available in several colors and textures by the sheet and in booklets.

Construction Paper is available in two weights: one is inexpensively priced and lightweight with a slightly rough surface; the other is moderately priced and mediumweight with a smooth surface.

Manila Paper, generally a buff color, is available in tablets and large sheets. Old file folders can be used as a substitute for manila paper.

Mat Board is available in large sheets and smaller cut pieces in a variety of colors, including metallics. This is a heavyweight paper, although it cuts easily with scissors and rotary cutters.

Newsprint, a lightweight paper, is available in tablets and by the roll. Very often your local newspaper will sell roll ends at a low cost. Some don't even charge for them—call around.

Origami Papers are available in several sizes, including 1″ squares, in a multitude of designs and colors. Some papers are colored on each side. Metallic papers have a plain paper backing and can be glued or fused to other papers and wood. The heavily textured types (Washi, for example) are not good for printing, although they are excellent to use for envelope liners or as trim.

Poster Board, a two-ply paper with a low-gloss finish, is available in several sizes and colors.

Shelf Paper (get Brand X) is one of the better papers to use for children's activities. The paper is economically priced, prints (and paints) well, and is easy to store.

Tracing Vellum is a translucent, nonabsorbent paper that is stronger than regular tracing paper. Purchase in fabric or sewing stores or from Sure-Fit Designs (see Appendix E).

ALPHABETICAL LISTING OF SUPPLY COMPANIES

With few exceptions, supplies and brands mentioned in the book will be available in local fabric, crafts, stamp, hardware and art supply stores. If a mail-order source is not given in a company's listing, contact the company for local purchase sources. It's not a bad idea to include a LSASE (large, self-addressed stamped envelope) with your request.

The mail-order catalogs listed for general categories in Appendix F (Arts and Crafts Supplies, for example) carry comprehensive supplies for that category.

Catalog prices were current December, 1993. However, rising printing and postage costs may affect future prices.

Accent
Borden Consumer Response
HPPG Division—Accent Products
180 East Broad Street
Columbus, OH 43215
(614) 225-4511

Adhesive Technologies, Inc.
3 Merrill Industrial Drive
Hampton, NH 03842

All American Graphics
2896 Colorado Avenue
Santa Monica, CA 90404
(310) 829-5909

Alpel Publishing
P.O. Box 203
Chambly, PQ J3L 4B3, Canada
(514) 658-6205
Flyer: Free with LSASE

Alpha Shirt Company
401 East Hunting Park Avenue
Philadelphia, PA 19124
(800) 845-4970
Catalog price: Free

American Art Clay Co., Inc.
4717 West 16th Street
Indianapolis, IN 46222

American Traditional Stencils
Mail-order source: Stencil Outlet

Artstampers World, Inc.
7558 58th Court East
Sarasota, FL 34243
(813) 351-8546
Flyer: Free with LSASE

Barrett House
P.O. Box 540
North Salt Lake, UT 84054-9585
(801) 299-0700
Catalog price: $2

Beadery Craft Products, The
105 Canonchet Road
P.O. Box 178
Hope Valley, RI 02832
(401) 539-2598

Bead It!
5242 North Clark Street
Chicago, IL 60640
(312) 561-9683

Dick Blick
P.O. Box 1267
Galesburg, IL 61401
(309) 343-6181
Catalog price: $3

Chartpak
One River Road
Leeds, MA 01053

Childcraft, Children's Growing Years
20 Kilmer Road
Edison, NJ 08818
(800) 631-5652
Catalog price: Free

Clotilde, Inc.
1909 S.W. First Avenue
Fort Lauderdale, FL 33315-2100
(800) 772-2891
Catalog price: Free

Clover Needlecraft, Inc.
1007 East Dominquez Street, Suite L
Carson, CA 90746

Createx Colors
ColorCraft, Ltd.
14 Airport Park Road
East Granby, CT 06026
Catalog price: $2

Creatively Yours
Loctite Corporation
North American Group
Newington, CT 06111

The Crowning Touch, Inc.
2419 Glory C Road
Medford, OR 97501
(503) 772-8430
Catalog price: Free with LSASE

DecoArt
P.O. Box 360
Stanford, KY 40484
(606) 365-3193

DEKA
P.O. Box 309
Morrisville, VT 05661

Distlefink Designs, Inc.
P.O. Box 358
Pelham, NY 10803
(914) 738-4807

Dharma Trading Co.
P.O. Box 150916
San Rafael, CA 94915
Catalog Price: Free

Delta
2550 Pellissier Place
Whittier, CA 90601
Customer Service: (800) 423-4135

Dizzle
Colortex Company
One Cape May Street
Harrison, NJ 07029

Dover Publications
31 East 2nd Street
Mineola, NY 11501
Catalog price: Free

Dritz Corporation
P.O. Box 5028
Spartanburg, SC 29304

EK Success Ltd.
611 Industrial Road
Carlstadt, NJ 07072-1687

Elementary Specialties
917 Hickory Lane
P.O. Box 8105
Mansfield, OH 44901-8105
(800) 292-7891; (419) 589-3600
Catalog price: Free

Elsie's Equisiques
208 State Street
St. Joseph, MI 49085
(616) 982-0449

F & W Publications, Inc.
1507 Dana Avenue
Cincinnati, OH 45207
(513) 531-2690
Catalog price: Free

FabricARTS
Ivy Imports
12213 Distribution Way
Beltsville, MD 20705

Fabricraft
Faultless Starch/Bon Ami Company
1025 West 8th Street
Kansas City, MO 64101-1200
(816) 842-1230
Pamphlet price: Free

Felt Gard
Shepherd Hardware Products, Inc.
Three Oaks, MI 49128

Fiskars Inc.
7811 W. Stewart
Wausau, WI 54401

Galacolor
1760 East 15th Street
Los Angeles, CA 90021
(800) Buy-Gala

Gare
P.O. Box 1686
Haverhill, MA 01831-2386

General Pencil Company
67 Fleet Street
Jersey City, NJ 07306

Gick Crafts
9 Studebaker Drive
Irvine, CA 92718
(714) 581-5830
Catalog price: Free

Grafix
Graphic Art Systems, Inc.
19499 Miles Road
Cleveland, OH 44128

Handcraft Designs, Inc.
63 East Broad Street
Hatfield, PA 19440

Joe E. Hicks, Inc.
1937 IH 35 East, Suite 106
New Braunfels, TX 78130
(210) 629-0994
Catalog price: Free with LSASE

House of White Birches
Berne, IN 46711
(800) 347-9887
Catalog price: $2

Jacquard
Information; Rupert, Gibbon & Spider, Inc.

Jo Sonja's Artist Colors
Chroma Acrylics, Inc.
205 Bucky Drive
Lititz, PA 17543
(717) 626-8866
Catalog price: Free

Kemper Tools & Doll Supplies
13595 12th Street
Chino, CA 91710
(909) 627-6191

Kony Bond
PDM Adhesives Corporation
133 Bethea Road, Suite 801
Fayetteville, GA 30214
(800) 248-4583

Liquitex
1100 Chester Lane
Easton, PA 18044-0431

L'Oiseau Bleu Artitsant
4146 Ste-Catherine Street East
Montreal, Quebec
Canada H1V 1X2
(514) 527-3456
Catalog price: Free with LSASE

Maiwa Handprints
6-1666 Johnston Street
Vancouver, B.C.
Canada V6H 2S3
(604) 669-3939
Catalog price: Free with LSASE

Mary's Productions
P.O. Box 87
Aurora, MN 55705
(218) 229-2804
Catalog price: Free with LSASE

Marvy Uchida of America Corporation
1027 East Burgrove Street
Carson, CA 90746

Master Magnetics, Inc.
P.O. Box 279
Castle Rock, CO 80104

Me Sew, Inc.
24307 Magic Mountain Pkwy., Suite 195
Valencia, CA 91355
(800) 846-3739
Flyer price: Free with LSASE

McGill Inc.
P.O. Box 177
Marengo, IL 60152

Nancy's Notions, Ltd.
333 Beichi Avenue
Beaver Dam, WI 53916-0683
(800) 833-0690
Catalog price: Free

NASCO
901 Janesville Avenue
Fort Atkinson, WI 53538-0901
(414) 563-2446
Catalog price: Free

Open Chain Publishing, Inc.
P.O. Box 2634ST
Menlo Park, CA 94026
(415) 366-4440
Catalog price: Free with LSASE

Palmer Paint Products, Inc.
1291 Rochester Road
Troy, MI 48083

Pearl All-Surface Fabric Paint
Mail order source: Pearl Paint Co., Inc.

Pearl Paint Co., Inc.
308 Canal Street
New York City, NY 10013-2572
(212) 431-7932
Catalog price: $1; minimum order required

Pebeo of America
Route 78, Airport Road
P.O. Box 714
Swanton, VT 05488
Mail order source: Pearl Paint Co., Inc. (Request Pebeo
Information Sheets)

Pebeo of Canada
1035, St.-Denis Street
Sherbrooke, QC J1K 257, Canada
Mail order sources: Maiwa Handprints; L'Oiseau Bleu
Artitsant

Peintex
Information: Savoir Faire

Plaid Enterprises, Inc.
P.O. Box 7600
Norcross, GA 30091-7600

Polyform Products Co.
9420 West Bryon Street
Schiller Park, IL 60178

Putnam Company, Inc.
P.O. Box 310
Walworth, WI 53184
(800) 338-4776
Catalog price: Free

Quilter's Rule International
2322 N.E. 29th Ave.
Ocala, FL 32670
(800) 343-8671

Quiltery
P.O. Box 5028
Spartanburg, NC 29304

Ranger Industries, Inc.
15 Park Road
Tinton Falls, NJ 07724
(908) 389-3535

Riverside Paper Co.
Appleton, WI 54912

Rowoco
2240 West 75th Street
Woodridge, IL 60517
(800) 772-7111

Rupert, Gibbon & Spider, Inc.
P.O. Box 425
Healdsburg, CA 95548
(800) 442-0455
Catalog price: $3

Sakura of America
30470 Whipple Road
Union City, CA 94587
(415) 475-8880

SASCO Supplies, Inc.
P.O. Box 10204
Erie, PA 16514

Savoir Faire
P.O. Box 2021
Sausalito, CA 94966

Sax Arts & Crafts
2405 South Calhoun Road
P.O. Box 51710
New Berlin, WI 53151
(800) 558-6696; in WI (800) 242-4911
Catalog price: $4; minimum order required

Scribbles
Duncan Enterprises
56732 Shields Ave.
Fresno, CA 93727

Setacolor (Transparent and Opaque)
Pebeo of America; Pebeo of Canada

Daniel Smith, Inc.
4130 First Avenue
Seattle, WA 98134-2302
(800) 426-6740 (U.S. & Canada)
Catalog price: Free

Speed Stitch
3113 Broadpoint Drive
Harbor Heights, FL 33983
(800) 874-4415
Catalog price: $3

Stencil Outlet
P.O. Box 80
West Notingham, NH 03291
Catalog price: $3

Sew-Fit
5768 West 77th Street
Burbank, IL 60459
(800) 547-4739
Catalog price: Free

Sure-Fit Designs
P.O. Box 5567-0567
Eugene, OR 97405
(503) 344-0422
Catalog price: Free

The Testor Corporation
620 Buckee Street
Rockford, IL 61104-4891
(815) 961-6654

Texticolor
Information: Savoir Faire

Therm O Web
112 West Carpenter Avenue
Wheeling, IL 60090
(800) 992-9700

Tower Hobbies
P.O. Box 9078
Champaign, IL 61826-9078
(217) 398-1100
Catalog price: $3 ($5 refunded with first order)

Transgraph-X
L J Originals
516 Sumac Place
DeSoto, TX 75115
(214) 223-6644

Treadleart
25834-1 Narbonne Avenue
Lomita, CA 90717
(800) 327-4222
Catalog price: $3

Tulip
24 Prince Park Way
Natick, MA 01760
(508) 650-4500

Tumble Dye
Seitec: Sew Easy Industries
2701 West 1800 Street
Logan, UT 84321

Viking Sewing Machine Company
11760 Berea Road
Cleveland, OH 44111
Brochure: Free

VWS
11760 Berea Road
Cleveland, OH 44111
Brochure: Free

Wagner Spray Tech Corporation
1770 Fernbrook Lane
Plymouth, MN 55447
(800) 328-8251

West Mountain Gourd Farm
Rt. 1, Box 853
Gilmer, TX 75644
(903) 734-5204
Information packet: $2

Westrim Crafts
P.O. Box 3879
Chatsworth, CA 91311

Wildflowers of Western Australia, Inc.
3010 South 96th Street
Tacoma, WA 98409

Wilton Enterprises, Inc.
2240 West 75th Street
Woodridge, IL 60517
(800) 772-7111
Catalog: $5.95 (Catalog also contains instructional material and usually is available in stores stocking Wilton products.)

Yasutomo & Company (Y & C)
490 Eccles Avenue
South San Francisco, CA 94080

Z-Barten Productions
8611 Hayden Place
Culver City, CA 90232

SUPPLY SOURCES

An alphabetical listing of supplies by type (for example, Acrylic Artist Colors) is given first and the companies selling those supplies follow. (Refer to Appendix G for names, addresses, and purchase information for stamp companies.)

Acrylic Artist Colors
Jo Sonja's
Acrylic Fabric Paint in Dabber Bottle
Ranger Industries, Inc. (Fabra-Ca-Dabra)
Acrylic Jewels, Mirrors
The Beadery Craft Products
Adhesive Vinyl (Quilter's Rule Clear Laminating Polyvinyl)
Available in quilt and fabric stores
All Purpose Sealer
Jo Sonja's
Arts and Crafts Supplies
In addition to supplies used for stamping, these catalogs carry a comprehensive array of products used for all arts and crafts activities:
Childcraft
Dick Blick
Elementary Specialties
NASCO
Pearl Paint Co., Inc.
Sax Arts & Crafts
Balsa Wood
Tower Hobbies
Battenberg Lace: Square Doilies, Yardage, Kits
Barrett House
Bead Easy Glass Beads, Bead Easy Glitter Adhesive, Bead Easy Clear Adhesive
Fabricraft

Blank Clothing, Accessories, Yardage
Alpha Shirt Company (cotton and cotton/poly clothing, and accessories)
Rupert, Gibbon & Spider, Inc. (cotton and silk clothing, blanks, yardage, and accessories)
Brush Pen
DecoArt (available in crafts stores)
Christmas Tree Skirt Batting
Putnam Company, Inc. (Special Edition)
Clay, Oven-Baked
American Art Clay Co., Inc. (Fimo)
Bead it! (Cernit)
Handcraft Designs (Cernit and Fimo)
Polyform Products Co. (Sculpey and Pro-Mat)
Compressed Sponges, Sheets and Precut Shapes
Joe E. Hicks, Inc.
Cooking Parchment Paper
Wilton Enterprises, Inc.
Craft and Needlework Supplies and Kits, Mail-Order Catalog
House of White Birches
Crafts Supplies: See Arts and Crafts Supplies
Craft Iron (Top Flite MonoKote Heat Sealing Tool)
Tower Hobbies
Craft Paints
Refer to brand name in Appendix F for mail order information; several catalogs listed under Arts and Crafts Supplies have many of the brands mentioned in the book.
Decorating Set
Kemper Tools & Doll Supplies
Design A Stamp
All American Graphics

Designer Dots
Kemper Tools & Doll Supplies
Draw & Saw
Grafix
Dried Flowers
Wildflowers of Western Australia, Inc.
Embossing Powders
Most stamp companies listed in Appendix G include embossing powders in their catalogs.
Ranger Industries (Foil, Tinsel, and Verdigris Embossing Powders)
Fabric Paints
Refer to brand name in Appendix F for mail order information; several catalogs listed under Arts and Crafts Supplies also have many of the brands mentioned in the book.
Fabric Stiffener
Fabricraft
Plaid Enterprises, Inc.
Fastube, Fasturn
The Crowning Touch, Inc.
Felt Pad Substitute
Felt Gard
Fiber Arts Supplies
Dharma Trading Co.
Flex Plate
Sax Arts and Crafts (Flex Plate is listed in catalog as Flexible Printing Plate)
Foil, Foil Glue
Plaid Enterprises, Inc.
SASCO
Fun Foam
Westrim Crafts
Glitter
Createx
Gick Crafts
Plaid Enterprises, Inc.
Z-Barten Productions
Gourds
West Mountain Gourd Farm
Heat Guns
Tower Hobbies
Wagner Spray Tech Corporation
Heat n Bond Original No Sew, Heat n Bond Lite
Therm O Web
Heat n Bond Iron On Flexible Vinyl
Therm O Web
"Hera" Marker
Clover Needlecrafts, Inc.
Hobby Supplies
Tower Hobbies
Identi-Pen
Sakura of America
Kiss-Off Stain Remover
General Pencil Company

Kitchen Shears
Rowoco
Laundry Detergent for Stamped and Painted Fabrics
Fabricraft
Light Tables
American Traditional Stencils
Me Sew, Inc.
Viking Sewing Machine Co.
Liquid Appliqué
Marvy Uchida of America Corporation
Magnet Sheets (with adhesive)
Clearsnap, Inc. (See Appendix G)
Master Magnetics, Inc.
Marker Glue
EK Success, Ltd. (Zig 2-Way Glue)
Kony Bond (2 In 1 Glue Marker)
Markers: Permanent, Watercolor
Marvy Uchida of America Corporation: Permanent and watercolor
Pebeo: Permanent
Sakura: Permanent (including White Opaque) and watercolor
The Testor Corporation: Permanent (enamel)
Yasutomo & Company: Permanent and watercolor
Zig: Permanent (including opaque) and watercolor
Mounting Film
Grafix
Mylar: Precut Shapes, Punched Ribbon, Spangles
Z-Barten Productions
Mylar Tape
Chartpak
Origami Papers
Yasutomo & Company
Peg Pop Mounts
Clearsnap, Inc. (See Appendix G)
Pen Score
Clearsnap, Inc. (See Appendix G)
Petifours
Plaid Enterprises, Inc.
Pillow Covers (bleached and unbleached muslin)
Putnam Company, Inc. (Soft Shapes)
Pillow Forms (Soft Shapes)
Putnam Company, Inc.
Positioning Tools: Stamp-O-Graph, Stamp-O-Round
Mostly Animals (see Appendix G)
Puff Additive for Fabric Paint
Createx Colors
Pearl Paint Co., Inc.
Pebeo
Puff Fabric Paint
Dizzle
Tulip
Repositionable Glues: Liquid, Marker, Spray
Liquid: Aleene's, Delta, Dritz, Fabricraft, and Plaid
Marker: See marker glue
Spray: Accent, Delta, and Creatively Yours

Rollers: Foam
Accent
DecoArt

Rollers: Hard and Soft Rubber (Brayers)
Available in crafts and art supply stores

Rotary Paper Trimmer
Fiskars, Inc.

Sequins; Sequin Glue
Distlefink Designs, Inc.

Sergers, Feet, Accessories
VWS

Sewing Machines, Feet, Accessories
Viking Sewing Machine Co.

Sewing Supplies, Mail Order Catalogs
These catalogs carry a comprehensive array of supplies
used for all sewing activities.
Clotilde, Inc.
Nancy's Notions, Ltd.
Speed Stitch
Treadleart

Silk Flowers, Ribbons, Trims
Elsie's Equisiques

Sketch Books
Riverside Paper Co.

Splatter Brush
Kemper Tools & Doll Supplies

Stencils
Brass
American Traditional Stencils

Colored Plastic
American Traditional Stencils
Delta
Gick
Plaid Enterprises, Inc.
Stencil House

Suction Cup Handles (for use on Sun Catchers)
Quiltery
Quilter's Rule International

Sunprint (Heliographic) Fabric Paint
Setacolor Transparent

Supplies for Making Fabric Paint
Createx Colors
Pearl Paint Co., Inc.

Syringe with Snap-on Top
Rupert, Gibbon & Spider

Texture Paste
Jo Sonja's

Tracing Vellum
Sure-Fit Designs

Transfer Ink (see Appendix E)
Comotion Rubber Stamps, Inc., Stamp `N' Iron Fabric
Transfer Ink
Ranger Industries: Iron-On Fabric Transfer Ink
Inkadinkado (See Appendix G)

Transfer Paint
DEKA Iron On Transfer Paint

Wipe-Out Tool
Kemper Tools & Doll Supplies

Wooden Boxes
Westrim Crafts

APPENDIX G

STAMP INDEX

Only a teeny fraction of the stamps available from the companies listed in this appendix were mentioned in the book. And these companies are only a teeny, tiny fraction of those that make and sell stamps.

It would take a book the size of the Manhattan Phone Book to include prints of every stamp mentioned. But each of those wonderful stamps can be seen either in a company's catalog or in stamp, crafts, and fabric stores.

If catalog information is not included in the listing for a company, that company does not offer mail-order sales to consumers at this time. Contact them for a local retail source where their stamps and stamping supplies are available.

Several companies offer unmounted stamps and assorted stamping supplies. That information is included in their catalog.

☛ **Note:** The "pointing hands" used on the title pages and on the first page of each chapter are NOT stamps but computer generated images. Stamps similar to these are available from several of the companies mentioned below.

Ad-Lib!
P.O. Box 1943
Burbank, CA 91507-1943
(818) 845-8180
Catalog price: $4.50 (unmounted stamp sent with catalog)

All Night Media, Inc. (ANM)
P.O. Box 10607
San Rafael, CA 94912
(415) 459-3013

Calico Cat Country Collection; Calico Cat Victorian Romance
See Majorstamps

Clearsnap, Inc.
P.O. Box 98
Anacortes, WA 98221
(800) 448-4862
Catalog price: $5

Comotion Rubber Stamp, Inc.
4455 South Park Avenue, Suite 105
Tucson, AZ 85714-1669
(602) 889-2200
Catalog price: $3

Craft House Corporation
328 North Westwood Avenue
Toledo, OH 43607

Delafield Stamp Company, Ltd.
514 Wells Street
Delafield, WI 53018
(414) 646-8599
Catalog price: Free

First Impression Rubber Stamp Arts
2100 NE Broadway, Suite 3F
Portland, OR 97232
(503) 288-2338
Flyer price: $2

Good Stamps.Stamp Goods
30901 Timberline Road
Willits, CA 95490
(707) 459-9124
Catalog and supplement price: $3

Graphistamp
Imprints Graphic Studio, Inc.
17371 NE 67th Court, Suite A-9
Redmond, WA 98052
(206) 867-5494
Catalog price: $3
and
Imprints Graphic Studio Canada, Inc.
200 Viceroy Road, Unit #10
Concord, Ontario
Canada L4K 3N8

Great Notions Rubber Stamps, Inc.
1210 3rd Street N.W.
Albuquerque, NM 87103
(505) 242-2633
Catalog price: $3, refundable with order

Hampton Art Stamps
19 Industrial Blvd.
Medford, NY 11763
(800) 229-1019
Catalog price: $2

ImaginAir Designs
1007 Woodland Ave. N.W.
Albuquerque, NM 87107
(505) 345-2308
Catalog price: $2, refundable with order

Inkadinkado, Inc.
76 South Street
Boston, MA 02111
(617) 338-2600
Catalog price: $3

Magna-Stamp
See Clearsnap, Inc.

Mail Order Marking (M.O.M.)
P.O. Box 997
Peck Station
New York, NY 10272-0607
(800) 345-6667, outside U.S. (212) 267-8797
Catalog price: $4 (makes custom stamps)

Majorstamps
2365 Monte Vista Street
Pasadena, CA 91107
(818) 795-5003
Catalog prices: Calico Cat and Victorian Romance, $3
each or $5 for both; Stamp.A.Quilt For Fabric, $5

Mostly Animals
P.O. Box 32266
San Jose, CA 95152

Museum of Modern Rubber (MOMR)
187-C W. Orangethorpe Ave.
Placentia, CA 92670
(714) 993-3587
Catalog price: $3

Neato Stuff
P.O. Box 4066
Carson City, NV 89710
Catalog price: $3

100 Proof Press
R.R. 1, Box 136
Eaton, NY 13334
(315) 684-3547
Catalog and supplement price: $4, refundable with order

Pelle's See-Thru Stamps (Pelle's)
P.O. Box 242
Davenport, CA 95017
(408) 424-4743
Catalog price: $2

P.O. Box Rubberstamps
1906 Ashland
Houston, TX 77008-3908
(713) 864-0656
Catalog price: $3.50

Quarter Moon Rubber Stamps
P.O. Box 611585
San Jose, CA 95161-1585
(408) 272-0211
Catalog price: $3

Raindrops On Roses
4808 Winterwood Drive
Raleigh, NC 27613
Orders (800) 245-8617, information (919) 846-8617
Catalog price: $3

Ranger Industries
15 Park Road
Tinton Falls, NJ 07724
Mail order source for alphabet stamps is Childcraft (see
Appendix E)

Rollagraph Stamp Wheel
See Clearsnap, Inc.

Rubber Stampede
P.O. Box 246
Berkeley, CA 94701
(510) 843-8910

Stamp & Design
See All Night Media, Inc.

Stamp.A.Quilt For Fabric
See Majorstamps

Stamp Affair
Hamilton Rubber Stamp Company
P.O. Box 7614
Round Lake Beach, IL 60073-7614
(708) 223-3339

Stamp Craft
P.O. Box 9737
San Rafael, CA 94912
(415) 455-8046

Stampendous
1357 South Lewis Street
Anaheim, CA 92805
(714) 563-9501

Sun Catchers
See Craft House Corp.

Stuck On Stamps (SOS)
A Division of Carda, International
P.O. Box 2539
San Antonio, TX 78299
(800) 255-9617
Catalog price: $2 (makes custom stamps)

Toomuchfun Rubberstamps, Inc.: Kate Darnell/Toomuchfun Rubberstamps, Inc.
515 East Grand River
East Lansing, MI 48823
(517) 351-2030
Catalog price: $3

Works of Heart
Mail-order source: Neato Stuff

BIBLIOGRAPHY

Periodicals

I think you'll enjoy each of these magazines—I know I do. Call or write for subscription rates.

The Artistic Stenciler
Stencils Artisans League, Inc.
P.O. Box 920190
Norcross, GA 30092

Crafts
News Plaza
Box 1790
Peoria, IL 61656
(800) 727-2387

Crafts 'N Things
P.O. Box 7519
Red Oak, IA 51595-0519
(800) 440-0441

The Creative Machine
Open Chain Publishing
P.O. Box 2634-ST
Menlo Park, CA 94026
(415) 366-4440

National Stampagraphic
1952 Everett Street
North Valley Stream, NY 11580

Quick & Easy Crafts
306 East Parr Road
Berne, IN 46711
(800) 829-5856

The Rebus Quarterly
P.O. Box 473 WOB
West Orange, NJ 07052

Rubberstampmadness
408 SW Monroe, #210
Corvallis, OR 97333
(503) 752-0075

Rubber Stampers World
1390 Broadway, Suite B153
Placerville, CA 95667

Sew News
News Plaza
P.O. Box 1790
Peoria, IL 61656
(800) 289-6397

Threads
63 S. Main Street
P.O. Box 5506
Newton, CT 06470-5506
(800) 888-8286

Wearable Crafts
306 East Parr Road
Berne, IN 46711
(800) 888-6833

Books and Booklets

Abel, Vista. *Imaginative Stamping.* Comotion Stamps, Inc., 1989.

All Night Media. *101 Ways to Stamp Your Art Out.* All Night Media, 1982.

Angeline, Christine. *The World's Best Stamp Book.* Mark Publishing, 1992.

bailey, elinor peace. *Mother Plays with Dolls.* E. P. M. Publications, 1990.

Brown, Gail. *Gail Brown's All-New Instant Interiors.* Chilton Book Company, 1993.

Burdett, Rosalind and Annette Claxton. *Gift Wrapping & Greeting Cards.* Gallery Books, 1990.

Crawford, Maureen. *Handmade Greeting Cards.* Sterling Publishing Co., Inc., 1991.

Fanning, Robbie and Tony Fanning. *The Complete Book of Machine Quilting.* Chilton Book Company, 1980.

Gleason, Kay. *Stamp It!* Van Nostrand Reinhold, 1981.

Gray, Bill and Jan Van Milligen. *Tips on Making Greeting Cards.* Design Press, 1991.

Hoover, Doris. *Too Hot to Handle? Potholders and How To Make Them.* Chilton Book Company, 1993.

Jackson, Paul. *The Encyclopedia of Origami and Papercraft Techniques.* Running Press, 1991.

Jackson, Paul and Vivien Frank. *Origami and Papercraft.* Crescent Books, 1988.

Kenzle, Linda Fry. *Embellishments: Adding Glamour to Garments.* Chilton Book Company, 1993.

Kitagawa, Yoshiko. *Creative Cards.* Kodansha International, 1987.

Laury, Jean Ray. *Imagery on Fabric.* C & T Publishing, 1992.

Miller, Joni K. and Lowry Thompson. *The Rubber Stamp Album.* Workman Publishing, 1978.

Mulari, Mary. *Travel Gear and Gifts To Make.* Mary's Productions, 1993.

Pellowski, Anne. *How to Make Cloth Books For Children: A Guide to Making Personalized Books.* Chilton Book Company, 1993.

Saddington, Marianne. *Making Your Own Paper.* Storey Communications, Inc., 1992.

Schoch, Vicky. *Embossed Paper.* Design Originals, 1992.

Directories

MAIL-ORDER CATALOGS

Two valuable books for crafters and stitchers list dozens (and dozens and dozens) of mail-order catalogs. One lists U.S. companies; the other lists Canadian companies. Each covers every subject from ant farms to stamps to zippers. The books can be purchased in bookstores and from the publishers.

U.S. MAIL-ORDER COMPANIES

Boyd, Margaret. *The Crafts Supply Sourcebook.* F & W Publications, Inc., 1992.

CANADIAN MAIL-ORDER COMPANIES

Albala, Lelia. *The Original Catalog of Canadian Catalogues.* Alpel Publishing, 1992.

STAMP COMPANIES AND STORES

This directory includes listings for the U.S., Canada, Europe, and Australia. It can be purchased in stamp stores and from the publisher.
Button, Roger. *Artstampers Worldwide Directory.* Artstampers World, Inc. 1993.

INDEX